Thinking about Preaching

Thinking about Preaching

Michael J. Townsend

✛ EPWORTH

Copyright © Michael Townsend 2007

The Author has asserted his right under the Copyright, Designs
and Patents Act, 1988, to be identified as the Author of this Work

British Library Cataloguing in Publication data

A catalogue record for this book is available
from the British Library

978 0 7162 0616 3

First published in 2007
by Epworth
4 John Wesley Road
Werrington
Peterborough PE4 6ZP

Typeset by
Regent Typesetting, London

Printed and bound in Great Britain by
William Clowes Ltd, Beccles, Suffolk

Contents

Introduction   vii

1 To Preach or Not to Preach?   1
2 The Preacher's Task   14
3 Approaching the Bible   25
4 Getting to Grips with the Biblical Text   38
5 Preaching and Christian Experience   53
6 The Preacher's Heritage   68
7 Preacher of the Faith   82
8 Preaching in Context   99
9 Variety in Preaching   112

Postscript   132
Resources   135

Introduction

This book is primarily intended for those who want to explore whether God is calling them to preach the Christian gospel. I wondered at first whether it needed a question mark in the title, so turning it into an invitation to those in such a position to reflect with me on the nature of the work to which they might be being called. But the act of writing it involved me in some significant reassessment of what I have been doing for over 40 years and hope, by God's grace, to be doing for a few years yet. In that sense writing it became a kind of personal refresher course. So I trust that it might also be of use to those who, like me, have been about this glorious task for a long time, but who would like to reflect on what they are doing in a very simple but fundamental way. It is a good thing for all preachers to think about preaching, however many years they have been doing it.

After more than 40 years in the preaching ministry I am still passionate about it. Despite all the criticisms which can be levelled against preaching as a means of communication in the twenty-first century, I believe that when it is done well, and with integrity, it nourishes and feeds the spiritual life of a Christian congregation as nothing else can.

People begin a preaching ministry in a variety of ways and at different stages of their lives. Mine began as a 16-year-old schoolboy, which looking back seems almost ridiculous to me now. What did I know about anything then? Yet I certainly had a sense that this was something to which God might be calling me, and the Church was sufficiently trusting and generous to allow that call to be put to the test and provided skilled and understanding people to act as guides and mentors. I have not kept the text of the very first sermon I ever preached, though I recall that it was given on the Sunday after Ascension (which was probably an unwise choice) and that it lasted exactly seven minutes! It is quite a salutary experience to look at old sermon manuscripts (I have kept all of mine except the first four). They are certainly a check on any tendency to pride, and they are also testimonies to the patience of the congregations who heard them, for I do not recollect ever receiving anything other than encouragement from those saintly people.

For ten years my preaching was done as a lay person, though for over 30 years now I have preached as an ordained presbyter of the Church of God. It is impossible to work out with complete accuracy how often I have preached, though a rough estimate puts it well in excess of 3,500 occasions at the time of writing. Quantity, of course, is not the point; it is quality that matters, but comments about that must be left to others! I would hope, though, that I have learned something about preaching from having done it on so many occasions.

Some of my preaching ministry has been relatively concentrated. This was so when I began preaching in the locality where I then lived and has been so again when, as a presbyter, I have been the minister to local churches. For two widely separated periods of my life I have had a less concentrated preaching ministry (a situation sometimes described, not entirely inaccurately, as 'hit and run preaching'). This was the case for four years as a ministerial student, when we were sent out on most Sundays to preach in different places; and then again during the 13 years I was a Methodist District Chair with responsibility for a relatively large geographical area. The result of all this is that I have preached in over 470 different churches, along with a few other settings such as school and college chapels and the open air. I would like to think that preaching to so many different congregations has also taught me something about preaching.

I am a Methodist who rejoices that we live in ecumenical days. Down the years I have also preached in (in alphabetical order) Baptist, Church of England, Congregationalist, Free Church of England, Lutheran, Presbyterian, Roman Catholic, Salvation Army and United Reformed places of worship. This is an experience that makes one aware, in all kinds of subtle ways, that congregations of different Christian traditions can have varying kinds of expectations of those who preach to them. I have tried to write this book in a way that is accessible to people from any mainstream denomination.

After all that, I am as enthusiastic about preaching as I was when I began, and I long to see it done as well as possible. This book is most certainly not the last word about preaching; that could, in any case, never be written. But it might be a first word and I have tried hard, with what success the reader must judge, to think myself back to the time I began and to the issues that buzzed around in my mind as I did so. I have been helped in this by having done quite a lot of work down the years with those who were just starting out on a preaching ministry, so their questions and issues have fed into my own thinking. I have deliberately written as simply as possible and have tried not to assume any significant prior theological study on the part of the reader. The numerous books on preaching which have a place on my study bookshelves have been consulted regularly, but they have not been discussed, and there is not a footnote or endnote in sight. I am, of course, very conscious that a huge number of complicated issues, theological, biblical and hermeneutical, lie just below the surface of what I have written, but I have tried my best not to yield to the temptation to discuss them. To have done so would have resulted in a very different book, one which I judge would have been less useful to its intended readership.

Nor is this a 'how to do it' book. The reader will find little or nothing in its pages about how to construct a sermon, and there are no handy tips on where to find suitable illustrations. Good practice hints do creep in from time to time, but by and large they are there to exemplify other points. The purpose of this book is to explore what it means to a man or woman to take on preaching responsibilities. What is the purpose of preaching? Do you have to be a particular kind of person to do it? What are the wells from which the preacher draws the water of life? How do preachers retain their freshness and enrich their ministry? These and related questions are at the heart of what is here. I hope, above all, that it conveys something of the excitement and enthusiasm about preaching that I still feel, though even after more than 40 years I have lost little or nothing of my feeling of apprehension on actually standing up to do it!

In one sense this book may be regarded as yet another of the many fruits of the ministry of the late Revd John Stacey. For a number of years he was the Local Preachers' Secretary for the Methodist Church of Great Britain. In that role John, who was himself a highly regarded preacher, offered inspiration, and quite a lot of challenge, to those exploring a call to preach. Early in my ministry he gave me strong encouragement to work with preachers, particularly fledgling preachers. I took that advice, and doing so has brought me much enrichment. So this book is dedicated, with gratitude, to his memory.

1

To Preach or Not to Preach?

In the mind of the general public the image of preaching is almost entirely negative. Preaching, at least as it has traditionally been done within the Church, ticks none of the boxes met with in courses on communication skills; 'Don't preach' will be a very basic bit of advice given during such training. In a multimedia age it is taken for granted that the 'talking heads' approach simply doesn't work (unless it is done deliberately and with the supreme skill of an Alan Bennett). Yet Sunday after Sunday churches all over the land feature a talking head – quite literally so if the sermon is delivered from a high pulpit, 'six feet above contradiction' as the old jibe has it. And yet, although preaching is, quite rightly, not without its critics, it does seem to work, there is no widespread movement among churchgoers for its abolition. By and large it appears to do the job for which it is designed.

Perhaps this is not quite so surprising. Worshippers remember a good sermon, not in the sense of being able to repeat its content or analyse its structure several weeks later, but in the sense of being encouraged in discipleship and drawn deeper into faith in some significant way. A story is sometimes told about a worshipper who said to a preacher, 'I can't remember anything of what you said last Sunday'. The preacher asked in reply, 'What did you have for lunch last Thursday?' When the worshipper admitted that she couldn't remember, the preacher commented, 'I expect it fed you at the time.' A sermon that was the vehicle for such spiritual feeding remains in the memory as

1

something for which to thank God even when the details have long been forgotten. Gratitude for sermons like that can be one of the many things that prompt people to consider whether God might be calling them to follow the same path, to become, in turn, someone through whom spiritual nourishment might be offered.

A 'call' to preach?

As soon as the issue is described in this way and the idea of 'call' has been introduced, new questions arise. For the most part the Church has taught that preaching is something that is undertaken by those who have a call or vocation from God for this particular work. This may come as part of a wider package involving other aspects of ministry and a vocation to ordination. Or it may come on its own, as a call to exercise the ministry of the word while remaining in one's secular employment. Either way it is about more than an individual deciding that it would be a good idea to become a preacher. The call needs to be tested by the community of faith to ensure, as far as this can be done, that it is a genuine call from God and not just the desire of someone with an outsize ego to inflict his or her views on other people. And the person who testifies to a sense of call, however hesitantly or uncertainly, needs to know that the faith community within which that calling will eventually be exercised will receive it and be supportive of it. Thus there is a process of discernment to be undertaken by everybody involved.

How does God call people, and how might anyone know with reasonable confidence whether or not they have received a genuine call from God? Some people say 'I just know', without being able to give any very coherent account of how that inner conviction arose or where it came from. Others can point to particular events and experiences which acted as a trigger for the initial thought. This might be as straightforward as another church member asking, 'Have you ever thought of becoming a preacher?' Some simply see the Church's need for preachers and recognize that it is within their competence to help meet that need. For others it is part of a call to a wider ministry, and preaching comes, as it were, as part of the job description (in which case the question of how a call is established as genuine applies to the wider ministry and not just the preaching). There are as many accounts of a call to preach as there are preachers. This should not surprise anyone, because God deals with human beings in this respect as in other aspects of their Christian lives, as unique individuals, made and cherished in God's own image.

However it comes and whatever account might be given of it, this sense of call is crucial for the preacher and the Church alike. It is worth pausing to reflect on the way in which this fact makes preaching different from almost any other activity. Christian people sometimes testify that they have a call or vocation to their daily work. Because we ought to live the whole of life as Christian disciples, not just the 'religious' part of it, that attitude is praiseworthy and right. But such testimony to a sense of call really says something about the attitude of the person making it rather than about the work itself. In itself the work might be done by anyone who has the skills for it, whether or not they would claim a call to do it and whether or not they have any religious faith.

Preaching is different; in a significant sense it is not a job for which we might apply. It would be perfectly possible to draw up a job description for preaching which would list the skills and abilities required to do it. There are plenty of people who would fulfil the criteria, teachers of religious studies or academic theologians for example, if they were skilled communicators and known to be committed Christians. But the person specification would need to include, 'Called by God to this work', and this is what makes preaching different. It is one of the mysteries of Christian life that on the one hand there are many people who would appear to be well qualified to preach but who never receive God's call to do so, while on the other hand there are people who become aware (in one of the innumerable ways in which it happens) that they may be on the receiving end of just such a sense of call, who then have to work very hard to attain the necessary skills. Often, those who feel called can scarcely believe what seems to be taking place in their lives, but set out in obedience to explore what it will mean for them.

A faith exploration

An exploration is precisely what is involved. There are no simple answers and there is no litmus-paper test which can be done to establish the genuineness of a call to preach. This should not surprise anyone. Discerning a call to preach is part of a faith journey both for the individual concerned and for the Christian community to which that person belongs. Like all other aspects of living by faith it requires of us that we set aside our very human wish for certainty and learn to exercise trust in God's goodness and the Holy Spirit's guidance. This is not always an easy thing to do, and it is rarely entirely straightforward. If we conclude that God is indeed calling us to preach we have to learn to trust that the inner resources to exercise that ministry will be given as and when they are needed. If we conclude that this is not, after all, God's call to us, we have to learn to trust that there will be some other way in which we can serve God and seek to discern what that is. Similarly for the Church: if someone's sense of call to preach is tested and affirmed, the faith community must, in faith, welcome and receive both message and messenger as from God. But if the call to preach is not affirmed the Church needs to support and encourage that person, trusting that other ministries will be opened up for him or her.

In seeking to discover or renew a sense of call to preaching it is important to reflect on what some of the barriers, both objective and subjective, might be.

Several very good reasons not to become a preacher

A lack of experience

When people preach they sometimes refer, directly or indirectly, to their own experience. Often this takes the form of a story or illustration. A preacher might describe something that has happened in her own life or in the life of her family and then talk about how that reveals God at work in daily living. Or he may share the conviction that at a particular point in time God spoke very directly to him, perhaps during a time of prayer, and will use that experience to encourage his hearers to believe. This kind of preaching often encourages and strengthens Christian people in their faith, so its value is known. There are also times when a preacher's story or testimony has been merely sentimental or else naive, and that can be rather embarrassing for all concerned. In either case we recognize that talking about Christian experience in this way involves some self-exposure. It means letting other people into some of the innermost recesses of our personality and laying bare those experiences that are very personal to us. If they are personal we are also inclined to think that they might be private. We might be willing to share such things with those close to us, where we know that they will not reject what we say or make fun of it. But talking about ourselves and our personal experiences in a safe way like that is very different from baring our soul, as it seems, in a public address.

On being good enough to preach

There is a related issue that might give us pause for thought. If, through preaching, something of the preacher's own understanding and experience of God is shared, does that not raise, in a quite probing way, the question of whether we are good enough to preach? Knowing ourselves as it is to be hoped we do, wouldn't we be, or at least feel like, hypocrites if we preached in public? The charge of hypocrisy is an easy stick with which to beat the Church and those who are seen to be speaking in its name. Hypocrisy occurs when people pretend to be living by the beliefs and values they preach but are actually doing quite the opposite. So if someone were to publicly proclaim the need for fidelity in marriage while all the time conducting an extra-marital affair in secret, that would be hypocrisy. Our real concern, however, will almost certainly be about something much more mundane, but still troubling. No doubt we try very hard to live by the faith we profess and pray to the Lord for grace to do so (which in itself exempts us from the charge of hypocrisy), but we are well aware that we are still sinful mortals and, as such, constantly fail in the attempt. This appears to create a contradiction between what we say and what we achieve. So, for instance, we can imagine preaching a sermon on Jesus' command that we should love one another. As we do so, in the back of our minds, we recall some occasion on which we behaved rather badly towards somebody else and we know that some people in the congregation are aware of it. Might they not be thinking, 'Who is she to preach to us about loving one another?'

In most churches – though not in all – the days when congregations expected preachers to be perfect ('Being good on our behalf' as it was once described) have long gone and we are the better for it. But there is an honourable tradition which says that those who lead the Christian community (and preaching is a significant way in which such leadership is exercised) should be 'examples to the flock'. There is even a biblical text which says that those who teach will be judged with greater strictness (James 3.1). If we feel, as most of us do, that our very ordinary lives of Christian discipleship hardly qualify us to be examples to the flock, ought that to disqualify us from preaching?

Then again, there is the question of whether we have, or can acquire, sufficient knowledge and understanding of the Bible and of Christian doctrine to use them in our preaching without making fools of ourselves.

Knowledge of the Bible

Preachers often take a passage from the Bible, perhaps even a single verse, and preach about what it means for believers today. Does this mean you have to be an expert on the Bible in order to preach? The Bible often seems so difficult to those who have never before studied it in any depth. There is a great deal of it, and much of it may seem either to lack obvious relevance to Christian living in the twenty-first century, or to be so obscure that nobody is quite sure what it means. Some Christians appear to know the Bible extremely well and quote from it frequently, but that can sometimes appear embarrassing to others, not least when it is done in a rather naive way.

We have our favourite passages and they may mean a great deal to us, but we don't want to become the kind of preacher who preaches predictable sermons from a few favourite passages. On the other hand, there are some preachers who seem very gifted at interpreting the Bible in their preaching. They can take even an unfamiliar passage and within a very short time that same passage speaks very powerfully about what God is doing in our world and in our lives today. We are conscious of being greatly blessed when this happens, but the thought of trying to do it ourselves can be quite frightening. We are also aware that though we read the Bible in our personal devotions and are often nourished by doing so, that is very different from trying to deliver a public message based on a book we may not understand very well.

It is also obvious that Christians do not always agree about what the Bible is, how to use it or what it means. Some claim to believe every word in the Bible literally and because of this argue that, for example, Christians must believe that God made the world in six days. Others appear to treat the Bible more like a resource book from which to pick and choose what to use. These issues can be deeply divisive even within a congregation. Those who are not preachers can keep their thoughts to themselves about such controversial matters, but preachers may have to put their heads above the parapet and can find themselves embroiled in unwelcome debate. This seems like an undesirable prospect.

Knowledge of Christian doctrine

Then again, preachers quite often find themselves needing to talk about what Christians believe. This is most noticeable at the big festivals such as Easter or Christmas when if the sermon had a title it might be something like, 'The Meaning of the Resurrection' or, 'The Meaning of the Incarnation'. And then there is always Trinity Sunday, when the sermon is often about that most confusing of subjects, 'God in Three Persons'. We may not feel very confident that we know enough about Christian doctrine to talk about things like this in ways which make sense on a public occasion. We may well have done our own thinking, even some reading about such things. There may have been opportunities to discuss what it is that Christians believe, perhaps in a house group setting, and such discussions have been both enjoyable and stimulating. But preaching is different. In some sense those who are authorized by the Church to preach do so on behalf of the Church; they are her official spokespersons. Preachers are not expected to offer just their own views, even though, of course, their preaching will be shaped by their own personality and insights – if it were not so preaching might

8

as well be done by robots. It seems like a big step from exploring what we ourselves believe, and being happy to discuss it with our friends, to becoming an accredited teacher of a great world faith.

Speaking in public

Preaching is a form of public speaking. This is most evidently so when the preacher is addressing a large congregation in the course of a formal act of worship, perhaps in a rather imposing building. It may appear less obviously the case when the preaching takes place in a small room with a couple of dozen people seated in a circle. Some small churches have, sadly, become accustomed to knowing who is likely to be in the congregation, even to the extent that the person on duty in the vestry says to the preacher, 'I think everybody is here now, so we can begin.' But even then preaching is still public speaking and it takes place in an act of public worship, usually advertised as such on the church noticeboard. Thankfully, there are still many congregations where new people are welcomed on a regular basis and where preaching feels, to preacher and hearers alike, as if it is a significant public utterance.

Unless we belong to that group of people who are sometimes said to like the sound of their own voice, most of us shy away, almost instinctively it seems, from engaging in any form of public speaking. A commonly expressed reaction to an invitation to do so, even in a modest way, is, 'I couldn't possibly do anything like that.' Even if we normally take pleasure in the art of conversation and enjoy expressing our thoughts when we are with family, friends or small informal groups, public speaking seems like a very different sort of activity – as indeed it is. It is understandable that the naturally diffident or shy might be reluctant to speak in public, but even people generally regarded as extroverts have been known to quail at the prospect of doing it.

There are, of course, exceptions to every rule; some people relish any and every opportunity of speaking in public whether or not they are any good at it. At one time or another most of us have experience of sitting through a lengthy speech which is boring, inappropriate or otherwise ill-judged, yet it has been all too obvious that the person delivering it is blissfully unaware of its effect upon the audience. The truth is, some preachers come into that category; the fact that something is said in church does not automatically make it worth saying. What, we may think, if *we* turned out to be like that, thinking that we were being interesting, thoughtful and relevant while all the time our hearers were bored out of their minds but far too polite, or full of Christian charity, to say so? This fear alone may make us hesitate to take up the task of preaching.

Obstacles and opportunities

So far we have briefly touched on some of the obstacles, objective and subjective, practical, intellectual and personal, which lie in the way of anyone who is considering becoming a preacher. Preaching demands a willingness to engage in what is often a quite formal public activity; for whatever reasons, we might never have thought that this is something we could actually do. Preaching seems to require a deep understanding of the Bible; we may not be sure that this is something that we have or could acquire. Preaching involves, in some form or another, authorization as an official teacher in the Christian Church; this is very different from any faith-sharing we might ever have done. Preaching entails sharing of personal Christian experience; this calls for a vulnerability which may make us uneasy. Preaching appears to set us up as a role-model for fellow Christians; we know our sins and failings too well to be comfortable about that.

In due course we will explore how these obstacles, and some

others, far from being the barriers to preaching that they might at first appear, actually uncover and offer resources which enable those who preach to do so in an authentic way. What seem to be obstacles can turn out to be opportunities. But first, we need to reflect on what might, at first sight, appear to be the greatest barrier of all to becoming a preacher.

An impossible task?

Christians do indeed make an astonishing claim concerning preaching; that it is a vehicle through which, in the context of worship, God is encountered and God's purposes are made known. It is, in other words, the principal way in which God speaks to the Church – and through the Church to the world at large. This is, of course, a statement of faith, utterly unprovable in any obvious sense. But it certainly resonates with the experience of Christian worshippers. Sermons change lives, open the door to new experiences of God's grace and love, evoke commitment, deepen faith and challenge limitations. The recognition that this is so is an awesome moment. How could any human being, no matter how clever, gifted or even holy, dare to take on such a responsibility? Certainly (for this is a very personal question and not just a theoretical one), how could *I* dare to do it? God's words on my lips – you must be joking!

The only good reason to become a preacher

The great twentieth-century Swiss theologian Karl Barth not only recognized this dilemma but gave particularly intense expression to it. He recognized that human beings, sinful and inadequate as they are, cannot even begin to speak of a holy and transcendent God without immediately misrepresenting the truth about such a God. He asked how, if that is so, we could dare to speak of God at all. His answer to his own question was

this: we do so only because God has spoken to us first, supreme-
ly through Jesus Christ who is the Word of God. In the very act
of calling us to faith God also calls us to be witnesses to that
same Word. So even though all our human speaking about God
is in one sense inadequate and distorted we have no choice but
to undertake it because our calling to discipleship is also a calling to witness.

Back to call

This brings us firmly back to the call and commission which
comes from God, which is the only good reason to become a
preacher. Some of the biblical stories about ways in which people were called to speak for and about God remind us that those
who took up the challenge were often very aware both of their
own limitations and of the awesomeness of the task. Many centuries before Jesus, Moses was called to lead God's people out of
their slavery in Egypt and was told to go to the Egyptian Pharaoh
with God's command, 'Let my people go.' His response, in effect,
was to ask the question, 'Who am I to do this?' and he received
from God the reply, 'I will be with you' (Exodus 3.11–12). When
Jeremiah became aware of a call to speak God's prophetic word
to people, he protested that he did not know how to speak in
this way. He then received what he described as the touch of the
Lord's hand upon his mouth (Jeremiah 1.4–10). Isaiah, another
prophet, famously lamented both his own unworthiness and
that of his people, and only after he had received cleansing and
forgiveness was he ready to obey the call to become God's messenger (Isaiah 6.1–8). According to the Acts of the Apostles the
risen Jesus told the assembled disciples that they would be his
witnesses even to the ends of the earth. Was that to be understood as a call, a challenge or a promise? In any case they would
have been incapable of responding to it without the promise of
the Holy Spirit's power with which it is coupled (Acts 1.8). So it

proved: the Church's preaching ministry began when the Holy Spirit came upon the disciples at the first Christian Pentecost.

These stories are a reminder that even if speaking God's word is an impossible task, it is one which God calls the Church, and specific individuals within it, to undertake. If God calls, and if we come to believe that the call has come to us, to turn our back on it would not be humility, it would be disobedience. The stories are also a reminder that with God's call come God's resources. The preacher's task is undertaken in conscious reliance on the Holy Spirit. That fact is never, of course, a substitute for study and hard thought, but it does mean that those who respond to the call may rely on God to guide their studies and their thinking. This, at least, should give some encouragement to those who feel overwhelmed by the task – and every genuine preacher who has ever lived has felt like that at some time or another!

2

The Preacher's Task

It is scarcely surprising that even experienced preachers can sometimes feel overwhelmed by what they are called to do. Or, to put it another way, good preachers never lose a sense of awe and amazement that God should have called them, with all their inadequacies, to such work. After all, it *is* an astonishing thing that God should entrust the announcement of life-changing good news to very ordinary human beings. At first sight this might appear to be a very good reason for not preaching. If it is as difficult as all that, and if the responsibilities are as great as they appear to be, perhaps it is best left well alone. Well, perhaps it is! But if we are to leave it alone, that needs to be done for the right reason, not for the wrong one. The right reason would be because after appropriate and prayerful reflection, perhaps after doing some training or having a go, it is clear that we are not being called by God to undertake it. The wrong reason would be because it appears to be difficult. Apart from anything else, there is the decisive consideration that the God who calls people to this vocation honours this call and enables it to be fulfilled. This is true for the process of training and formation as a preacher and it is also true as sermons are prepared and preached. Preachers learn, gradually of course, to look at life differently just because they are preachers. This is not to say that everything becomes merely sermon fodder, but if, as the Jesuit poet Gerard Manley Hopkins puts it, 'The world is charged with the grandeur of God', then the whole world is grist to the preaching mill.

Up to this point a great deal of emphasis has been placed on the awesomeness of preaching. There is a good reason for this. Preachers who think of themselves as just giving a little talk of no great significance or as reading an academic essay to the congregation can end up diminishing the Christian gospel, even though this is not what they intend. When good news is replaced by good advice and the wine of the gospel has been changed back into the water of a cosy chat, something vital is missing, God's people are then not nourished and the life of the Church turns in on itself. It is therefore essential that all who preach understand from the beginning, and keep in mind throughout their ministry of preaching (perhaps each and every time they preach), that what they are doing is nothing less than providing the means through which the Word of God (Jesus Christ) is made known to those who hear.

The other side of the awesomeness coin, as it were, is surely an exciting sense of privilege. There is, after all, no other message like the good news of the Christian faith. The story of God's love for each and every human being, good news for bad people (as well as for those who think of themselves as good and not in need of it), is the best story there has ever been or could ever be. To be called to have a part in telling it, to offer God's invitation to faith and its renewal in daily life, is a huge privilege and exercising it often brings great joy.

All that said, it is very important not to become grandiose or pretentious about preaching. It may be awesome in the sense already referred to, but it happens! Sunday by Sunday thousands of ordinary men and women accept this responsibility and carry it out, often very well. The ultimate goal of preaching may be awesome, but the practical task which faces the person who is going to preach is, on the face of it, much more mundane – it is to write something called a sermon! Now that might appear a bit daunting, especially for those who have never done it before, but it is clearly not impossible. It is at one level a definable, measurable responsibility. So, what is the nature of this sermon which needs to be written? What kind of writing is it? Is it like writing a lecture, or a lesson or an essay? Or like writing a company report, a sales pitch or a journalistic commentary on the state of the world? Or is it something else entirely?

What is a sermon?

The dictionary definition

One well-known online dictionary defines a sermon as 'a part of a Christian church ceremony in which a priest gives a talk on a religious or moral subject, often based on something written in the Bible'. It also offers a definition which carries with it a sense of disapproval: 'a long talk in which someone advises other people how they should behave in order to be better people'. This second definition needs no further consideration. It is merely a reminder of what has already been noted in Chapter 1 – that preaching usually has a somewhat negative image in the popular imagination. No one who is seriously involved in preaching, as either a practitioner or a hearer, would think, even for a moment, that a sermon is primarily designed to advise other people how to behave.

The first definition is objective and neutral, as is entirely proper in a dictionary. What a reader would not take away from it is any sense of what a sermon is intended to achieve, nor, therefore, any sense of the potential importance of preaching. A sermon may well be 'a talk on a religious or moral subject', but why is the talk being given in the first place? What is it intended to convey and what difference does the person delivering it hope it will make?

A specific objective?

Those whose job it is to make speeches or give talks and addresses in a secular context often have a specific objective in mind when they do so. At one time it was standard advice in 'how to do it' textbooks for beginners in preaching that every sermon should have a single clear aim which the preacher would do well to jot down before beginning to write the sermon and then keep in mind throughout the process. So, for example, the sermon manuscript might be headed, 'Aim: to encourage people to pray more faithfully'. At one level this was probably quite good advice if it encouraged the kind of clarity of thought which makes it easier for a congregation to follow what is being said. At another level it was very bad advice because it encouraged sermons to focus on particular topics, perhaps setting out an argument, reaching a conclusion and, as it were, asking the congregation to agree with it. But an argument is not an invitation nor is it, in itself, news of who God is and what God wants for us. So it might end up hardly being preaching at all. Perhaps before beginning *every* sermon what preachers should really write at the top of the manuscript is along the lines of: 'Aim: to speak of things in a way that makes it possible for us to meet with God'. This would faithfully reflect preaching's origins in God's word spoken to us through Christ, and it would also remind the preacher that within such an aim a considerable variety of ways of speaking can be grist to the mill. Sermons are, after all, both like and unlike other ways of talking with which we might be familiar; so if we are to preach, some reflection on this might be useful.

Preaching informs, but . . .

Talks that offer nothing except factual information are increasingly thin on the ground these days. If information needs to be shared it can readily be done in printed or electronic form through photocopiers, scanners and emails and can be filed and kept for reference as needed rather than having to be remembered. Much information-sharing would be quite bizarre if it took place through speech. It would be absurd for the Operations Manager of the local bus company to deliver a public address on 'Forthcoming changes to our routes and timetables' instead of causing new timetable leaflets to be printed and distributed. Nevertheless, talks and addresses can often be described as information-based; those who hear them need to be given, or perhaps reminded of, certain facts before they are in a position to respond. We can imagine that a Chief Executive might address the monthly meeting of Area Sales Managers on the trends in sales for the various product ranges the company sells. No doubt the basic information will be available at the meeting in the form of tables of statistics and in graphs and charts, with the whole thing repeated on Powerpoint. But the Chief Executive knows that *hearing* the figures conveys them with an initial impact not quite achieved by any other medium. In the same way, although a good teacher does a great deal more during a lesson than impart factual information, some of that does take place. One of the decisions teachers must make is about how to be selective with their information. They need to try to ensure that their students are in possession of the key facts about an issue and, most importantly, have some idea of why they matter. It is sometimes said that 'everybody remembers a good teacher', and, in most people's experience, the good teachers they remember are those who were genuinely enthusiastic about their subject and had the gift of communicating that enthusiasm to those whom they were teaching.

So preaching does need to inform its hearers, at least to some extent. Preachers often find themselves sharing information with their congregations, not least biblical information. There has been a dramatic decline in biblical literacy among the population as a whole, despite 72 per cent of the population of Britain describing themselves as Christians in the 2001 census (and we recall that since preaching takes place in public worship people may be present who have little grasp of even the basic Christian story). Sadly, despite the variety of Bible-reading schemes and notes that are available, there appears to have been a decline in biblical literacy within the Church as well, though to nothing like the same degree. Preachers of the past could afford to allude in passing to biblical stories and the doctrines of the faith. Those who take on the preaching task today find that it involves some basic education, though as a tool, not as an end in itself.

Preaching persuades, but . . .

In one way or another most talks are ultimately intended to persuade the hearers to believe in something or to think and/or act in a particular way. The classic example is a politician's speech. A government spokesperson may reel off statistics about the number of new schools and hospitals that have been built and the number of new teachers and medical staff who have been employed, but the primary purpose is to persuade us that the government is doing a really good job in those areas and that we should therefore vote for them when the opportunity next arises. Those who speak for opposition parties seek to persuade us that the government is not doing as good a job as it claims and that their party would do a great deal better if we, the voters, give them the opportunity next time. It is important to note that much of the public cynicism about politics today is actually generated by this kind of speaking. Everybody knows that information can be distorted and statistics can be made to say anything, so people are not always impressed when they are quoted, even when they are correct. Quite unfairly in many cases, that cynicism often extends to motives. Politicians are rarely believed when they claim to have entered politics because they wanted to make a difference to society. The public attitude is sometimes expressed in the phrases 'they're all the same' and 'they're all in it for what they can get'. This means that when people speak in order to persuade others the reaction may be that the hearers just wonder what is 'in it' for the speaker.

In principle there is nothing wrong with wanting to persuade others of the rightness of the way we see things; we do it all the time. A sermon would be rather strange if it did not attempt to do this – at the very heart of preaching is the desire to see those without faith come to it and those with faith deepen it. But those who take up preaching find they need to be careful about the way in which it is done. The issue for would-be preachers is, what kind of persuasiveness springs out of gospel values and Christian spirituality? In the life, death and resurrection of Jesus what we see is God's *invitation* to relationship (sharing in a great feast, as some of the Gospel parables describe it). So preaching must offer that same invitation and do so in the same gracious way. It does not bludgeon people, it does not force people to see things in a particular way; rather, it echoes the Psalmist's call, 'O taste and see that the Lord is good' (Psalm 34.8). In doing so it respects the integrity of the hearers and recognizes that even though God does all things well, that particular achievement is beyond the grasp of any preacher.

This means that although a preacher needs to have confidence about calling, he or she also needs to have humility about content. Preachers certainly attempt to persuade, but do so in ways, and perhaps with a demeanour, which would be thought odd from a politician. Perhaps what people often find difficult about politicians is an unwillingness to admit that they might not have fully understood a situation, that they have got something wrong or that they simply don't know the answer to a problem. The persuasiveness of a preacher leaves room for all those possibilities. Preacher and people alike are on a pilgrimage in which further study, reflection, prayer and action will bring greater light. Those who take on the preaching task today find that they need to learn how to persuade, but to do so in humble love.

Preaching is personal, but . . .

Most of us find other people's lives interesting and we like hearing and reading about them. Biographies and autobiographies are, it seems, among the most frequently borrowed books in public libraries. Scanning the annual programme for the local Soroptimists, Probus Club, or any other organization that regularly invites outside speakers to its meetings, will reveal the regularity with which people give talks about what they do, or have done, either in their working lives or as a hobby. Since people do not talk about their work unless they are deeply committed to it, or have a hobby at all except for the same reason, such talks inevitably reveal a great deal about the speaker's character and personality, outlook and relationships. Which is why, of course, they are so popular. There will often be an element of education in all this, though the primary purpose is perhaps entertainment in the widest sense.

In some respects a sermon is personal, though not quite in the way in which the talks that have been referred to are personal. Christianity is not an abstract religion. The faith that is proclaimed through preaching does not consist of a set of propositions, proposals or policies that can be learned and put into practice. At the heart of Christian faith is the story of God's dealing with humanity and, most particularly, of the way in which God became incarnate as a human being in the person of Jesus Christ. The New Testament Gospels record (though not in the same manner as a modern biography would do) the way in which Jesus lived out his life and gathered others around him in a community. Since that time, Christian believers have attempted to live by the light of the story of Jesus. Christian history is the record of their successes and failures in doing so. If the Christian story is about God's dealings with people, then stories of the people with whom God deals (including the preacher) are important.

The primary aim of a sermon can never be entertainment, even in the widest sense. Entertainment is directed at the pleasure of those who see and hear it, but its essence is that it demands no commitment from anybody. Entertainment does not usually aim to change anything (with the exception of some alternative comedians whose comedy does set out to challenge attitudes and prejudices). The sermon, on the other hand, aims for commitment and would wish not to leave its hearers essentially unchanged by the experience. Those who take on the preaching task today need to tell the story, their own and that of others, in order to earth what they are saying in the joys and sorrows that come with being human.

Preaching gives vision, but . . .

Leaders are looked to for vision. One of the most important qualities in a leader is the capacity to think on a large scale, to have vision about where things should be going and the capacity to communicate that vision to other people.

Sometimes people offer vision for the organization that they lead, so a head teacher might share with the staff at the beginning of the school year a vision of what kind of school she wants it to be and how that vision might be fulfilled. More widely, a politician might make a speech that sets out a vision of what kind of society (or even world) he wants to see and of how his party or government intends to try and bring it about. Such occasions are intended to generate enthusiasm and energy for what needs to be accomplished and to draw forth commitment from the hearers. When a piece of work is difficult or demanding, and especially if things are not working out in the way that might have been hoped, it is easy to become weary, to put in less energy and commitment, even to be tempted to give up. What people need in that situation is to be put back in touch with the very things that brought them to take up the cause in the first place in the hope that this will rekindle their enthusiasm for it.

The Christian faith is undeniably visionary in the sense that it sets out a vision of how the entire world might be if the reign of Christ was seen and God's intention in creation was fulfilled. It is unlikely that anyone would wish to take up preaching in the first place if they lacked all appreciation of that glorious possibility, however imperfectly they may grasp it. So although a sermon may not often speak directly in visionary terms, such vision will always be there as a kind of backcloth to everything else that is said.

Congregations need to know this, or at least sense it. Because living the Christian life is often quite difficult and there are a number of discouragements and setbacks to deal with along the way, there is constant need for recharging of the spiritual batteries, which a good sermon should provide. Those who take on the preaching task today need to learn how to share the vision in ways which help people move on.

Preaching springs out of the gospel

In the light of what has been discussed we may pick a small quarrel with the dictionary definition of a sermon that was quoted towards the beginning of this chapter! Part of it runs: ' . . . a talk on a religious or moral subject, often based on something written in the Bible'. The problem with this definition is with the way in which it contrasts the words 'moral' and 'religious', as if they are two different, or at least independent things. This implies that a satisfactory sermon could be preached on a moral topic without any reference to religion, but this cannot be right. It is, of course, perfectly possible to give a talk on, say, 'The morality of nuclear power' without any reference to religion, and many valuable things might be said during it. But it would not be a sermon and it would not belong in Christian worship. Whatever subject is dealt with in a sermon, it always has to spring out of the gospel word, God's revelation in Jesus, and reflect the challenge this brings to us. Preaching, we remind ourselves, is never advice of any kind, it is always news – news of what God is like and of how we can become more Christ-like in respect of some aspect of our lives. Those who take on the preaching task today learn to make connections!

Summing up the preacher's task

At its best a sermon will offer people a vision of what God wants for them and their world, a gracious invitation to engage with God in ways which will help them to bring that vision to fruition, enough information to make informed choices, encouragement to persevere and the assurance that Christian discipleship is undertaken in company with others, including the preacher. This means that the preacher, in conscious reliance on the Holy Spirit, becomes the vehicle for God's story to become real in the lives of the hearers, so that they are caught up in it and respond. If the process of becoming a preacher who can fulfil that role and who can deliver sermons which do that seems rather intimidating, it is important to continue remembering the resources which a calling and caring God has promised to provide. It is to these that we now turn.

3

Approaching the Bible

Pre-eminent among the resources which God has provided for preaching – and indeed for the life of the Church as a whole – is that collection of books and writings which we call the Bible. This may seem a surprising statement. Isn't it rather odd, and certainly inadequate, to describe the Bible as a resource? Surely in the context of preaching, a resource is something which people may choose to use, or otherwise? We can hardly imagine that such an option exists with regard to the Bible! Indeed not, and if the Bible is to be thought of as a resource it needs to be remembered that it is very much more. At the very least it is the primary and indispensable resource for the Christian preacher and some aspects of that fact will be explored in due course. Nevertheless, it may not be unhelpful to begin thinking of the Bible as a resource, partly because Chapter 1 alluded, fairly briefly, to some of the reasons why the Bible might at first sight appear to be an obstacle to taking up preaching. It contains many wonderful things, but it also contains some things that are extremely difficult to understand, others that are a source of disagreement among Christians and yet others that appear to be totally irrelevant to Christian living today. Preachers must learn to see this huge book as God's ultimate resource, rather than as a hindrance. How might this be done?

The Bible says ...

One busy Saturday afternoon, street-preaching was taking place in one of the precincts of an English city. A small group of people were standing together, each holding a large Bible. One of their number started to preach: 'The Bible says that God has sent his Son Jesus Christ to be the propitiation for your sins.' None of those passing by appeared to be even remotely interested in this news. It probably wasn't the word 'propitiation' that turned people off, though it is a word we might well hesitate to use in public. It was that *any* sentence beginning with 'the Bible says' immediately tells those around that what follows has nothing to do with them. Despite its international bestseller status it is virtually unread outside the Church in twenty-first-century Britain. A term that is sometimes used to describe preachers (though it can be applied to Christians who are not preachers as well) is 'Bible-basher'. The only two things which most people think they know about the Bible are that 'you can prove whatever you want to' from it and that, in the words of Sporting Life from George Gershwin's *Porgy and Bess,*

> De t'ings dat yo li'ble
> To read in de Bible,
> It ain't necessarily so.

The street-preacher, attempting to reach the unconverted, needed to reckon with this and amend his preaching accordingly if he was to have any chance of his good news being heard. The difficulty, almost certainly, was that *for the preacher* 'the Bible says' carried great weight and would clinch any argument. He probably found it difficult to understand that this was not the case for others. What about those who will normally preach, not in precincts and on street corners, but in pulpits and from behind lecterns during services of Christian worship? They may appear to be preaching to the converted, as the saying goes (though that will not always be true). How much authority does 'the Bible says' carry for the converted?

In practice, there is a wide range of opinions within most Christian denominations concerning the authority of the Bible and the way in which it is to be used. At one extreme is the view that the Bible is the complete and only authority for faith and conduct because its human authors were conduits for the word of God. A preacher who sees the Bible in that way will seek to discover what it teaches and then urge congregations to believe it and obey it. At the other extreme is a view that we have to disregard most of what the Bible says because it comes from another age and social situation, but that it offers some passages of great spiritual wisdom of which account should be taken. A preacher who sees the Bible like that will no doubt preach accordingly.

The very phrase 'the authority of the Bible' needs a little teasing out. The word 'authority' itself is quite a complicated one. It often denotes power and control over people's lives and conduct through the making of decisions or the issuing of orders by those who have the right to do so. An example of this would be a decision by a customs officer to search someone and their luggage if there was reason to suspect that illegal substances were being brought into the country. But the word also signifies the possession of expertise of a high order. An example of this would be if the government needed to put measures in place to protect public health in the face of a threat to it. Views would be sought from the person who is thought to know most about that particular threat and how it can be contained, someone who is considered an 'authority' on the subject and whose opinions can be safely taken as definitive. Yet in neither instance is this authority absolute or beyond dispute. The person being threatened with a search by a customs officer could challenge that authority if it could be shown that there was no reasonable suspicion of wrongdoing and the search was being conducted purely on the officer's whim. Another expert on the threat to public health could express disagreement about whether the first person's view was correct and therefore definitive. In democratic societies anyway, authority can only ultimately be exercised because it receives the consent, either explicit or implicit, of those who are subject to it.

This must also be true of the way the Bible's authority works within the Christian community. The Bible does not, in itself, have the power to make anybody do or believe anything. If it has authority for people that is because it has proved itself to convey the life-giving word of God afresh in each generation in a way that nothing else does, or could do. In a little while we will reflect on some of the reasons why that is so. For the moment it is sufficient to note that Christians *choose* to put themselves under the authority of the Bible.

All this may begin to seem a bit bewildering, even a little off-putting. After all, many people who are wondering about a call to preach have never had any real reason to think through, in such an abstract way as this, what they believe about the authority of the Bible. Surely it isn't necessary to have worked through such issues before beginning to preach? No, indeed it isn't. In some ways it may be better *not* to have done so. Growing experience in actually handling the biblical material and in preaching from it, along with the biblical studies which form part of every preacher's training, are important factors in helping to shape someone's eventual views about what kind of authority the Bible has. Initial uncertainty about this rather complicated matter is no bar to exercising the calling. In any case, a far more important issue for preachers is how the biblical material is actually used in preaching. Preachers learn how to say what the Bible says and (which is more important and not always quite the same thing) what it means, without ever saying, 'the Bible says'!

The centrality of the Bible

Whatever theoretical definition of the Bible's role in faith and conduct may be held, the simple fact is that almost all Christian denominations place the Bible at the centre of worship and the heart of preaching. The dictionary definition of a sermon that was quoted early in Chapter 2 noted that sermons are 'often based on something written in the Bible'. This reads like a fairly neutral observation, which is what we expect from dictionaries. It does not say that sermons *ought* to be based on something written in the Bible, but it does claim that they 'often' are and it is right to do so. For example, changes in the pattern for worship in most major denominations in recent years have had as one of their principal aims to bring the Bible readings and the sermon into a closer relationship with one another, rather than having the readings in the middle and the sermon at the end, as was once widely the case. Putting readings and sermon together emphasizes that in the Church's view the latter *ought* to spring out of the former.

But why is this so? Why should a collection of writings, the newest of which is almost 2000 years old, occupy such a central place in worship and preaching today and be considered of such importance? If Bible readings were replaced by passages from contemporary spiritual writers and if the preacher was encouraged to speak only about contemporary Christian concerns, what would be lost?

God's story – the preacher's story

The Jewish actor David Kossoff (1919–2005) was also known for his skills as a storyteller, particularly with regard to the Bible. In 1971 he published his best-known book about the Bible, which also became a television series, and perceptively called it *The Book of Witnesses*. That is a superb description of the Bible, and one from which preaching can spring. The biblical writers bear witness to God's words and actions at particular times and in particular places. In other words, they tell God's story. This makes their writings uniquely valuable, irreplaceable and, for those who need to know what God is like, impossible to ignore. The passages from contemporary spiritual writers which might possibly be read in church instead of the biblical lessons could not, if they are Christian, ever have been written if it were not for the Bible. They are always derivative and therefore secondary. And if (as occasionally happens) they are not Christian, they ought not normally to be read in Christian worship. The biblical writings are the primary source for what we know of God's story, nature, actions and demands. This is why the Church calls them the Holy Scriptures ('scripture' just means 'what is written', it is the adjective 'holy' which is important here). The preacher therefore needs to know, love and use these foundational documents.

When the Church decided which writings should be included in the New Testament (it sometimes comes as a shock to people to learn that it was the Church which decided this, but it was so), a number of different criteria were applied, not always totally consistently. One of these was called 'apostolicity', by which was meant, 'Does this writing go back in some significant sense to one of the original apostles?' Some of the arguments which were used seem a bit odd to scholars today and some books which are now in the New Testament very nearly were not, while others, of which few today have heard, very nearly were. Well, the early Christians prayed for the guidance of the Holy Spirit! But their concern for 'apostolicity' means that they too saw the importance of these writings as authentic witnesses to the story of God.

Take the Gospels as examples. By including the four which are in the New Testament and excluding a number of others (some of which make very interesting reading), the Church was claiming that in these particular writings is to be found what people need to know about Jesus in order to come into a relationship with God through him. This was not a claim about the accuracy of everything they record (how could it be when they sometimes differ among themselves?). It was a declaration that these writings are authentic witnesses, they offer truth and they are bearers of life. Therefore, Christians believe these writings as a whole to be normative for their faith and practice. They are the starting-point for everything that can be said (and therefore preached) about God.

In an important sense there is nothing to be added to these ancient texts. Just as the Church believes that the essential nature of God was made known in the life of one particular person who lived in Palestine, suffered under Pontius Pilate, was crucified, buried and raised on the third day, so it believes that the essential witness to God's truth is made known in one collection of writings that it calls Holy Scripture. Those who preach engage in an act of witness, but the story they tell is wholly dependent upon that primary book of witnesses, the Bible. This is a huge resource for the preacher simply because the Church (and through the Church the Holy Spirit?) assures us of the authenticity of this witness.

Based on the Bible

Preaching will, therefore, normally be closely related to one or more of the biblical readings. Some denominations use a scheme of readings (known as a lectionary) by way of either requirement or encouragement. In that situation the preacher knows beforehand which lessons are appointed to be read. While this can at first appear to be a constraint or even a frightening prospect, it is actually quite liberating. When a sermon begins, the congregation does not know what will be said, what word of life and faith from God is going to be presented to them. Congregations that are good listeners (they generally become so by being regularly given preaching that nourishes them) listen expectantly. The preacher who is dealing with a biblical passage that is relatively or even totally unfamiliar is in much the same position when the sermon preparation starts. She or he has to learn to listen attentively to what the passage is saying, which generates a sense of being *encountered* by God's word through that scripture. This is a healthy state of affairs because those who speak through preaching need first to listen to what God is saying. Those who have some experience of preaching know that a sense of surprise while preparing the sermon is a regular occurrence ('Goodness me! Why have I never seen that before?'). The preacher is also the first hearer of the sermon.

In some Christian traditions preachers are expected or allowed to choose their own biblical readings in public worship. This can be a quite difficult thing to get right. It is relatively easy at certain times of the year, especially at the major Christian festivals such as Easter, Pentecost and Christmas. But where does one start to find readings for a Sunday morning in August? Opening the Bible at random would not seem to be a very commendable course of action! The great temptation is to opt for those passages that are familiar and well loved, that one has already thought about, or that have already spoken powerfully in the preacher's Christian journey. Yielding to this temptation for the first few sermons one ever preaches would be understandable, but it ought to be resisted thereafter. It can be quite difficult to come to such passages of Scripture with open ears and fresh minds and, therefore, harder for the preacher to hear God's word for the congregation through them. At worst this can lead to preaching which is merely cosy, where it is evident to all that the preacher has not really been encountered by Scripture. If the preacher is required to select the readings for the service then that obligation cannot be shirked, but it is important not to run too readily to the familiar. As it happens, there is probably no reason why the preacher who is expected to choose the readings should not opt for those in the lectionary! Although churches of some denominations do not normally expect a lectionary to be followed, and others have a lectionary which is optional, nobody actually *forbids* the preacher to use the lectionary readings on a given Sunday if she or he wishes to do so. They can, at least, provide a starting-point.

How the preacher handles the actual biblical text that lies open before him or her as a sermon is prepared, and how, and with what intention, the Bible is *used* in sermons is another matter, and some attention will be given to that in the next chapter. Before it is possible to do that, it is necessary to reflect on the need for budding preachers to acquire some sense of the Bible as a whole. If its various writings tell, as they do, the developing story of God's love, in many different contexts and ways, some appreciation of what might be called the thread or line of that story is important. This is not because any given sermon will attempt to tell the whole of that story (perish the thought and pity the congregation!), but because the particular part of the story on which the sermon is based needs to be understood within its total context. No doubt all believers would benefit from seeing the story as a whole, but for preachers it is indispensable.

The whole story

The call to preach is often heard by those who have not previously done any really serious study of the Bible. That does not mean that they have not taken the Bible seriously. Quite the contrary; they are likely to have seen the Bible as very important. It is quite possible that God's call was first discerned through a word of Scripture. But acquaintance with it that is largely based on hearing it read in church services or through daily devotional readings, possibly accompanied by explanatory notes of some

33

kind, will not have given a sense of the sweep of the entire biblical witness. Approved lectionaries may well cover an astonishing
amount of the Bible over a three-year cycle, but they necessarily
do so in small chunks. The closest most congregations come to
appreciating the wider picture is in those churches where, on
Palm Sunday, the whole of one of the Passion stories is read. In
churches which do not use a lectionary, where the responsibility for choosing the readings lies with the preacher, it is likely
that the Bible will be read even more selectively! Congregations
can easily get a somewhat unbalanced picture of the Bible as a
whole and what they rarely, if ever, receive is a sense of what the
Bible is about overall – why this collection of writings has been
brought together between two covers – and therefore of the
sweep of its message. But, as has been noted, this is something
the preacher does need to acquire in order to understand the
particular material that is being dealt with on a given Sunday. A
grasp of this, even in a very simple sense, builds the preacher's
confidence because it gives the bigger picture. How might this
be done?

Where to begin

If we imagine someone saying, 'I want to know about Christianity, so I want to read the Bible; where do I begin?' what would
be the sensible reply? Though there are people who like to read
the newspaper backwards (perhaps because they find the sports
pages the most interesting ones), the normal practice with a
book is to start at the beginning and read through to the end.
Anyone putting that into practice with the Bible would find the
opening words, 'In the beginning', very encouraging. However,
within a few verses our imaginary reader would be plunged into
a story which says that God created the world from nothing in
six days. Questions are immediately raised in the reader's mind:
How could this be so when science says differently? What kind

of writing is this? The story of Adam and Eve, the first human beings, then follows. Our imaginary reader, almost certainly brought up on the theory of evolution, would not know how to interpret this beautiful story and might abandon the Bible (and Christianity along with it) at that point. Even if he or she persevered, many pages then follow concerning the growth and development of a Near Eastern tribe, including a lot of very detailed instructions about how they should offer animal sacrifices and a good many rules about how to behave in a society very different from the one in which we live. Although there are some fascinating stories and wonderful characters to be met with in those pages, it isn't at all obvious how they have anything much to do with being a Christian today.

It is evident that you cannot satisfactorily obtain a sense of the thread of the story and of the overall scope and sweep of the Bible by beginning at the beginning and reading through to the end. The reason for this is, of course, that although the Bible is bound between two covers, it is not one book or writing, but many (Christians are not all agreed on the exact number, but there are 66 of them in the versions usually used in Protestant churches in Britain). Our imaginary reader ought to have been told to begin not with the first, but with the most important. That would also be true for novice preachers.

Since the Christian faith is centred upon Jesus Christ, the proper place to begin is with those books that tell the story of Jesus, the four Gospels: Matthew, Mark, Luke and John. It would be quite helpful to read them in the order in which most biblical scholars think that they were written: Mark, Matthew, Luke and John. What is even more helpful is to read through each of them in turn at one sitting. None of the material is unknown and some of it is very familiar indeed. We will almost certainly have heard it all read in church at some time or another and read a great deal of it personally, especially if we use a Bible-reading scheme. But to read a Gospel in its entirety begins to give an overall sense of what the writer of that Gospel believed God was doing for the world through the life, ministry, death and resurrection of Jesus. Indeed, this is an exercise which can also be usefully undertaken by very experienced preachers.

Those who read the Gospels in this way quickly become aware that the Gospel writers were not merely recording events, they were also interpreting those events for the reader, through the way they write. The author of John's Gospel is quite explicit about this. Towards the end of the book he writes: ' . . . these (things) are written so that you may come to believe that Jesus is the Messiah, the Son of God, and that through believing you may have life in his name' (John 20.31). Although the other Gospel writers do not spell it out quite as explicitly as that, it is plain enough that this is their purpose also. An ancient name for the Gospel writers is 'the Four Evangelists' – which means that they are also preachers!

How to continue

The most natural question to ask, on reaching the end of one of the Gospels, is, 'What happened next?' or even, 'What did God do next?' Fortunately, the Bible contains a sequel (usually thought to be by the same writer as Luke's Gospel), called the Acts of the Apostles. This relates the story of the coming of God's Holy Spirit upon the disciples of Jesus and how this turned them into preachers, with the consequence that they and their converts became the founding members of the Christian Church of which we are part today. This book also introduces us to the character of Paul, who was very influential in helping to think through exactly what it was that God did through Jesus Christ and what it means for the world. His writings about those issues are also found within the covers of the Bible.

To begin with the Gospels, in the centre of the spectrum, and then move through the Acts of the Apostles and even into Paul's letters is to move forwards in time and development. But what about backwards? Isn't it equally important to know what lies behind the Gospel stories and the story of Jesus himself? It certainly is, and an attentive reading of any of the Gospels (Matthew's in particular) will leave a reader with a lot of unanswered questions in this respect. It is clearly very significant that Jesus is a Jew and, on occasion, he is recorded as quoting from, or referring to, the Jewish Bible (which we generally call the Old Testament, though the term 'Hebrew Scriptures' is becoming increasingly used). There are some stories in the Gospels whose meaning seems to depend on the reader having some knowledge of those scriptures. Unfortunately, although there is a book of the Bible that tells us how the story of Jesus is continued (the Acts of the Apostles), there is no such book in the Bible that tells us what lies behind it. What the preacher needs at this point is a reliable though not over-detailed scholarly summary of the story of the people of Israel (some resources for this are mentioned at the end of the book). For Christian readers (Jewish readers would see it differently of course), Jesus is the culmination, even the fulfilment, of that story. It cannot be fully understood without him, nor he without it.

Once a would-be preacher is equipped with this wider perspective it will be a real confidence booster because it provides a kind of scale or continuum for the biblical writings into which, for the most part, individual characters and writings can be fitted. Even so, some very important questions about the preacher and the Bible still remain: How, for example, does the preacher deal with the actual biblical text that lies open before him or her as a sermon is prepared, and what is the preacher's responsibility to the congregation so far as that text is concerned?

4

Getting to Grips with the Biblical Text

The preacher's calling, then, is to discern the word from God which lies within the Scripture readings for the day – however they have been chosen – and then to speak that word in inviting ways which will enable members of the congregation to hear it as well and respond to the presence of the living God in their midst. How do preachers set about this task?

Pray hard!

It may be stating the obvious, but the first and most important thing is prayer. Most novice preachers do not need to be told this; faced with a blank sheet of paper or computer screen, a passage from the Bible and a sermon to prepare for next Sunday, nearly everyone will pray! But we need to be reminded what such prayer is really about. There are preachers (perhaps fewer than there used to be) who claim never to prepare in any way other than praying hard and long about what they should say. Presumably they believe that if it is God's message they are to deliver then God can be expected to give it to them in answer to such prayer. A story that has long been current in preaching circles concerns a worshipper who, after a service, asked the preacher how long the sermon had taken to prepare. On receiving the reply, 'I just pray about things and the Holy Spirit tells me what to say', the long-suffering worshipper commented, 'Well, please tell the Holy Spirit he was particularly boring this morning.'

Prayer is never a substitute for careful preparation, any more than it is a replacement for action in any other part of Christian living. The preacher's prayer is that God will help him or her to hear and understand what the Scriptures are saying, to be sensitive to the needs of the congregation and to use well the skills and gifts that are brought to the undertaking. Countless preachers can testify to the fact that God honours such prayer. Those who do not yet have sufficient personal experience of preaching to have discovered this for themselves can take heart from the testimony of others. This kind of praying does not belong only to the beginning of a preaching ministry, it always needs to be part of the warp and woof of sermon preparation. For some more experienced preachers there is a very real danger of becoming blasé about this, of thinking, even subconsciously, that there is no need to pray directly about what is being undertaken. Practice in preaching never makes perfect, but it does, inevitably, lead to certain skills and techniques becoming so well honed over the years that they can be applied and used without very much conscious thought. Good preachers never lose a sense of awe about what they are doing, often still accompanied by trepidation when the moment comes to stand up and preach. What does usually disappear, however, is the sense of mild panic that, in the early days, can be generated by the combination of a blank sheet of paper or computer screen, a passage from the Bible and a sermon to prepare for next Sunday. If the disappearance of that also involves the fading away of the need to pray, something vital has been lost. The prayer should not be driven by the panic; it should arise out of awareness that if this is God's work that is being embarked upon it needs, quite naturally, to be soaked in prayer. The preacher's prayer does not just precede the preparation, it accompanies it throughout.

The preacher and the text

The previous chapter offered the reflection that Bible-based preaching is about allowing the word of life and faith which God has for this particular preacher and congregation to be heard through the Scriptures. This is not quite the same as saying that the preacher's task is to 'bring the Bible alive' for the congregation, although that will almost inevitably happen if the word is indeed heard. Nor is it quite the same as saying that the preacher's task is to help the congregation 'understand' the biblical passage concerned, though their deeper appreciation of its meaning will be an almost inevitable outcome. Rather, the sermon's purpose is to become the means through which worshippers can encounter the Scriptures for themselves, and thus hear and respond to the gracious invitation that God offers in Christ through the biblical text. In order for this to happen for the congregation it has first to happen for the preacher.

Getting at meaning(s)

The preacher's primary responsibility to the text (and the congregation) is to dig into the meaning of the biblical passage(s) under consideration. But before beginning to think about how this might be done, some words of caution are in order. As we grow up and learn to read, it is simple unambiguous language that we first encounter: 'The cat sat on the mat.' It is not capable of any other interpretation. When we have learned to read this text we know beyond argument that a cat is being referred to, not a dog, that the cat in question did not lie or stand but sat, and that it sat not on the chair but on the mat. And, of course, we continue to meet such simple unambiguous language all our adult lives: 'No Parking', '8 items or fewer at this checkout'. But it isn't very long before the child who has read something more complicated that he or she hasn't understood asks, 'What does that mean?' For all sorts of reasons it may not be possible to give a very simple answer to that question. But the child has grasped a very important distinction: we may understand what something says easily enough, but grasping what it means by what it says is a different and often more complicated matter.

As adults we become used to the intricacy of human thought and to the language that expresses it. With this comes the recognition of the impossibility of pinning down complex thoughts and convoluted arguments in language as simple and unambiguous as 'No Parking'. Experience teaches us that it is not sensible or helpful to assume that any complex written material carries just one fixed and unalterable meaning that has only to be discovered in order for us to know for certain and for ever what it 'means'. Most writing, certainly nearly all of the Bible, is more multifaceted, and interesting, than that. It is therefore slightly odd that people occasionally approach the Bible as though it is largely made up of absolutely clear and unequivocal material. What the Bible (or any particular part of it) *says* may very well appear to be clear and unequivocal, but what it *means* may be another matter.

The preacher therefore mines the biblical material in the same way as interpreters of any other kind of literature will approach their particular genre, not to look for a single fixed meaning, but to allow it to display the several layers of meaning that any living text contains.

The basic questions

In the first place there is the very important question of what the author intended to convey (some literary scholars think this isn't a significant question at all, but that approach makes ulti-

mate nonsense of all human communication). It is often helpful, occasionally even necessary, to have some help from biblical specialists and to consult biblical commentaries and the
like – but that comes later in the sermon-writing process rather
than at this point. In the second place there is the issue of what,
in the light of the author's intended meaning, the passage might
mean for us now. Getting from the one to the other is a matter
of discernment and making connections.

The third main concern for the preacher mining a biblical passage is: What assumptions and presuppositions do we
(preacher and congregation) bring to this text? Does a white,
middle-class, well-educated male preacher see the sayings of
Jesus about poverty and wealth, for example, differently from
the way a black woman from a deprived background and with
little formal education would see them? The obvious answer
is yes, but for most of the time we are not consciously aware of
the assumptions we make; they are simply part of who we are
and how we see life. The questions we ask of a passage reflect the
concerns and issues of our daily lives, and the answers we look
for are those that will help us in that context. This will almost
certainly be very different from the context in which the text
was originally written. What we are doing is not illegitimate,
but we need to have our eyes open to what we are about. This
is just another of the many layers of meaning that the text will
reveal to us.

Perhaps all this talk of complexity and uncertainty sounds
rather off-putting. If a would-be preacher has never done any
serious biblical study, and has perhaps thought that preaching
was largely a matter of discovering what the Bible says and then
teaching that in the sermon, it may well be. But if mining the
meaning of a biblical passage is not quite as straightforward
as might have been imagined, it is also more exciting! So there
is no need to be discouraged – far from it. Most preachers have
found that this astonishing book of witnesses we call the Bible,

though it does not always yield up its meanings quickly and simply, has an astounding capacity to convey new meanings for fresh situations and needs. If, as Christians claim, its witness is to the God who is as alive today as in the days when it was written, this is only to be expected. The Bible itself does not change, how could it if the core and essential witness to God's truth is made known through it? But that is not quite the last word on the matter.

In 1609 a group of Puritan Christians left Britain for Holland, in search of greater religious freedom. Their pastor and spiritual leader was called John Robinson (1575–1625). In 1620 a minority of this congregation decided to join the famous group now known as the Pilgrim Fathers in their journey to America. Robinson, who stayed behind in Holland, addressed them as they assembled. He said, 'I am very confident that the Lord hath yet more truth and light to break forth from his holy word.' Time and again, preachers prove the truth of that well-known statement. So inexhaustible is the Bible that the preacher may be confident of never coming to an end of what God offers through it. When a passage in the lectionary readings comes round again (three years later in most cases), experienced preachers sometimes look back to see how they preached about it on the previous occasion. Only rarely will the sermon be thought preachable again as it stands. In the intervening period the preacher has changed, as have the world and the congregation – even if they are the same people. As the preacher looks at the passage again, new insights come and fresh thoughts are generated: the Lord provides fresh truth and light from the words of the Scriptures. This is a reason to rejoice.

Getting into the text

The first thing the preacher needs to do is to read the passages through very carefully. That might appear a very obvious thing to say but, particularly in the case of a familiar passage, it is easy to assume that we know it already: oh yes, the parable of the Good Samaritan – everybody knows that! But familiarity breeds, if not exactly contempt, certainly staleness. The preacher needs to come to Scripture as freshly as possible in order to be surprised and challenged by it. To read the passage carefully is a good start. Assuming the would-be preacher knows neither Hebrew nor Greek (the languages in which most of the Bible was written), this is best done using two or three different translations, preferably as unlike one another as possible. Most people have a favourite translation and to use other, less familiar ones, can provoke questions that might otherwise not have arisen, about what the passage is saying. In any case, there is an Italian proverb that comes out in English as 'all translations betray' – which they do. No one translation of the Bible can possibly begin to do justice to all the shades of meaning that are found in the original. The process of comparing two or three gets the preacher closer to the layers of meaning to be found in the Scriptures.

Paying close attention

When David Isitt held the post of Director of the Bristol Diocesan School of Ministry in the 1980s he pioneered a method of Bible study that was called CAT – Close Attention to the Text. In 1989 he described the process as one in which ' . . . the students were required to look hard at a selected passage from the Bible and learn to read the scriptures closely, with a view to expounding them responsibly and intelligently'. It sounds just the ticket for the apprentice preacher! It has the supreme virtue of encouraging preachers to do their own basic work on a biblical passage *before* consulting the various commentaries and other aids that are available. This is very empowering. Of course, like anything else that is worthwhile, it requires practice. With such practice comes the art of knowing which questions to ask – for CAT is essentially about asking questions concerning the text in front of us and seeing what answers it gives.

Perhaps the first question to ask of any biblical passage is: What *kind* of writing is this? Is it a story about someone, or a story that someone tells to others? Is it an argument, a poem, a slice of history, or something else again? Once we are as clear in our minds as we can be about that, it is possible to go on to ask other questions through which the text can begin to uncover its secrets. It is important to recall the two basic concerns with which the preacher will approach any biblical passage: (a) what, so far as it can be discerned, the author intended the reader to understand by this passage; and (b) what, in the light of the author's intended meaning, the passage might mean for a contemporary Christian. What follows are only some *possible* questions relating to these two concerns. As a preacher develops confidence in handling biblical passages, he or she can expect to develop a method of questioning that is more personal and, therefore, more fruitful.

If the passage is a *story about someone* we might ask under (a): Why is this person acting in this way? Who else is involved in the story? What is the effect of what happens on people around? Is there any indication that the location in which the story takes place is significant? Are there any words provided that seem to interpret the story? Does it remind us of any other stories we can remember from the Bible? Why does the writer place it at this particular point in the book? What, if anything, does this story tell us about God and in what way is it good news? And we might ask under (b): Does anybody today act like this, and what would be the effect if they did? How would someone need to act today to achieve the same result as we read about here?

If it is a *story someone tells to others* we might ask under (a): To whom is this story being told? Why do they need to hear it? What are the reactions to it? Why does the writer place it at this particular point in the book? What, if anything, does this story tell us about God and in what way is it good news? Under (b) we might ask: What, if anything, gets in the way of this story conveying its message today? Are there any contemporary stories that would convey the same meaning? Who needs to hear the point of this story today, and why? What, if anything does this story tell us about God and in what way is it good news?

If it is an *argument* we might ask under (a): To whom might this argument possibly be addressed? What, if anything, might have happened to cause this passage to be written? How important does the writer believe his argument to be; is the writing passionate or casual? What might those who appear to disagree with it say in reply? Does this passage contain the whole of the argument, or is there more elsewhere? Why does the argument come at this particular point in the book? Some questions under (b) might be: Is this issue of any significance today and, if so, where and in what way? Are there any contemporary issues to which this line of argument might apply? What, if anything, does this argument tell us about God and in what way is it good news?

If it is a *poem* we might ask with respect to (a): To whom might this be addressed? Why do we think the poet wanted to write it? Is there something here that could not have been expressed in any other way? Under (b) we might consider: Does this poem speak to us now? If it does, what are the reasons? Is there any contemporary literature that performs the same task, or does the language and imagery of this poem still 'work'? What, if anything, does this poem tell us about God and in what way is it good news?

If it is a *historical account* we might ask (a): What is the significance of the events being narrated? Does the writer take a view about whether these events are praiseworthy or otherwise? What is the effect of the events upon the people most directly involved? Is there any hint about the longer-term effects of what has taken place? And under (b) we might ask: What, if anything, does this narrative tell us about how human actions accomplish lasting good for humanity, or otherwise? Are there any parallels with events in recent history? What, if anything, does this story tell us about God, and in what way is it good news?

The above method is, of course, only one possible way of beginning to get to grips with what the text has to say to us. Practising it, or something akin to it, enables the apprentice preacher (and indeed the experienced preacher as well) to recognize that we have within us the capacity to begin mining those meanings in Scripture that will enable us to preach life-giving sermons. This is in no way to belittle formal training in preaching, which is hugely valuable, or the contribution to sermon-making that is made by the biblical scholars and commentators, whose work should be consulted on a regular basis. Rather, it involves developing gifts that neither we nor our congregations may have known we possessed, but that are implicit in a call to preach. We might be surprised by them, but God knew of them all the time, which is why we have been called to preach!

It may well be that giving such close attention to the biblical text will provide the preacher with as much material as is needed, perhaps even more than is required, for the shaping of the sermon. The preacher who reaches the end of this exercise with a sense of what the passage means and of its relevance to Christian discipleship in the contemporary world has the bones of the sermon ready to hand. But what if that has not happened? It is important to be realistic: some scriptures are more difficult and intractable than others. It is possible that the questions that we have asked of the text do not have obvious answers, or we are simply bewildered about what the answers might mean. It is time to consult the experts.

Commentaries and other helps

Even if a close reading and rereading of the passage has yielded plenty of useful material it is still useful to consult the experts – it if hasn't, it is essential. Biblical study, like any other branch of human knowledge, is a vast subject, and if you go into it very thoroughly it can become extremely technical. Perhaps this is the reason why some Christians are wary of biblical scholarship. They suspect that it makes things even more confusing than they were before and they may fear that scholars will undermine what they regard as their 'simple faith'. Such a fear is largely groundless. Many biblical scholars are themselves believers and do their work as part of the community of faith, hoping that it will be helpful to other believers. In any case, what kind of a faith is it that cannot withstand examination and questioning? So the would-be preacher should not fear consulting the experts, indeed should welcome and embrace the help they can offer. Such help comes, broadly speaking, from two sources.

The first source of help of which the apprentice preacher is likely to become aware is the lectionary commentary, several of which are available online. These are usually based on the most commonly used lectionary known as RCL (Revised Common Lectionary). They group together the appointed lessons for the day and then offer comments and other thoughts on each of them. There are several good reasons for turning to this kind of resource. One is that they are usually written specifically with preachers in mind, so the writers usually try to provide the type of material a preacher will find helpful. Another advantage is that they can help the preacher deal with the sometimes puzzling question of whether the sermon should be based on just one of the readings (in practice this is usually the Gospel), or on two or even all three of them. The compilers of the lectionary sometimes select readings where there is a relationship of subject or theme between two or more of the readings, but on other

Sundays there is no such intended relationship. The preacher can waste precious time by trying to find a relationship where none exists! These kinds of resources, by putting the readings for the day side by side and offering comments on each of them usually make this much clearer.

The disadvantage of such lectionary commentaries is that they can tend to spoon-feed the preacher rather more than is desirable. Ideally, they should be used primarily as a check on the work the preacher has already done, though they are undeniably very useful in providing a kind of kick-start when the preacher's own work has become stuck. The important thing is that, like any other resource, they should never become a substitute for the preacher's responsibility under God to work with the text. Some further thoughts on lectionary commentaries can be found in the resource section.

The second major resource in this area is the commentary on a biblical book or books. By and large this is a genre of writing with which those who have never done any formal biblical studies are unlikely to be familiar. For the preacher they ought to become frequently consulted friends and, indeed, indispensable. There are some 'one volume' commentaries that cover the whole Bible (or in some cases just the New Testament) between two covers. These can provide general information, but they are not detailed enough to assist the person who wants help with a particular passage. What is really required is a single-volume commentary on just one biblical book (though this term also covers those commentaries that deal with several shorter books, such as the Minor Prophets or the Letters of John). In those, the author has sufficient space to deal with the issues the preacher wants to know about. Quite often the author will ask the same kinds of questions the preacher has already asked, but will have greater background and other knowledge through which answers can be found. The preacher might have struggled with a question such as, 'Why does the writer place this story at this point?' but the commentator is usually able to offer some helpful thoughts on such matters.

Some biblical commentaries are written from a strictly academic standpoint. They are intended to be read by other scholars and by those studying for educational qualifications in theology. They are not quite what the preacher needs. On the other hand, there are commentaries that are written from what might be called a 'devotional' perspective (many daily Bible reading notes come into this category), and those are not quite right either. What the preacher needs is a commentary that does its best to help the reader understand what the biblical text means without becoming too technical about it. Some of the best of these also include consideration of how the passage might speak in a wider context, including that of believing and living the Christian faith today. Preachers would find it helpful to build up a library of such commentaries, beginning with those books of the Bible from which sermons are likely to be preached most frequently. Some further thoughts on this can be found in the resources section.

A temptation to be resisted

Most people exploring a preaching ministry will already be aware that there are a number of websites, along with some books and journals, which offer not just commentary material but complete sermons on the readings for each Sunday. They are extremely tempting, especially if we are finding the biblical passages really hard going and there doesn't seem to be much light at the end of the tunnel. Many of these sermons are written by very capable and experienced preachers. Perhaps they will get us started. Why not make use of the gifts God has given to them?

The reason why not is that, especially at the beginning of a preaching ministry, they can damage one's own preaching abilities. The great danger is that, having read such a sermon and recognized how good it almost certainly is, we yield to the temptation to customize and adapt it a bit, and then preach it as our own. But it is not our own and it never can be! Implicit in God's call to preach is that each person who is so called brings to the task his or her particular personality, skills and gifts. The importance of this cannot be over-estimated. It would be possible, in theory, for each denomination to appoint a national sermon-writer who would produce a sermon for that week and distribute it to all the churches, where it could be read aloud. There would then be no need for preachers! There are a number of reasons why the Church does not do things that way, but chief among them is the conviction that 'sermons' of that kind would lack authenticity. Real preaching comes out of the way in which individuals who are called to preach do so out of the (developing) resources God has given to them. The end result might be less impressive from a technical standpoint than the work of a national expert would be, but it is real and authentic, which alone gives life. Perhaps, just perhaps, the preacher who has developed confidence that his or her own 'voice' as a preacher has begun to be established (say a minimum of ten years' experience), might risk taking a peek at someone else's sermon on next Sunday's readings, just in case there is a good illustration that might come in useful. Perhaps.

And finally . . .

Once the preacher has prayed, read the text carefully and thoroughly and interrogated it, prayed, used those resources that are available and prayed again, what next? The wise preacher tries to follow the advice of the Lutheran biblical scholar Johann Bengel (1687–1752), who wrote: 'Apply yourself wholly to the text; apply the text wholly to yourself.' Applying the text wholly to themselves takes preachers beyond the interpretation of the Bible and into the world of Christian living.

5

Preaching and Christian Experience

The second part of Johann Bengel's dictum, 'Apply the text wholly to yourself,' is a reminder to all preachers that they live under the word. The act of preaching can never be an example of the maxim 'do as I say and not as I do', for that would be hypocrisy.

Living under and by the word

One of the most precious things any preacher brings to the work is that person's own Christian discipleship as it is being lived out at home, at work, in the neighbourhood and among the congregation. Nobody knows better than ourselves what failures we often are as would-be followers of Jesus (well, perhaps our nearest and dearest sometimes do!). Yet other people will certainly recognize that we are far from perfect. Unless we are grossly insensitive (in which case we ought not to be preaching in the first place) it can be an unnerving experience to stand up on a Sunday morning and realize that in front of you is a congregation that may include people with whom you may have had a public row, or whom you have offended or treated badly in some way, however unintentionally. Every preacher faces some degree of resistance to being heard, created by his or her personality and other people's reaction to it. The African proverb, 'I cannot hear what you say because of what you are' needs to be remembered with genuine humility by all who preach. And, since other people usually do not know the half of it, as we say, our own awareness of our inadequacy in the life of faith certainly plays its part in our attitude to what we do and our willingness to do it.

As was suggested in Chapter 1, this may be one of the reasons for experiencing real reluctance to make a commitment to a ministry of preaching in the first place. Sometimes congregations place those who preach on a kind of spiritual and moral pedestal, perhaps because they genuinely assume that is where the preacher belongs, or perhaps because they have a psychological need for some kind of role-model – who knows? Whatever the reason it is a profoundly unhelpful thing to do. Apart from anything else, it can create a situation where, albeit subconsciously, members of the congregation end up reacting to challenging things they have heard in the sermon by thinking, 'Well, that's all right for you because you are a preacher, but it doesn't really apply to the rest of us.' It is even worse if the preacher, again quite possibly subconsciously, colludes with such a mindset. If a preacher does in fact end up as a role-model for members of the congregation, that is God's business, not the preacher's. No preacher should ever expect or seek such a situation. And yet, as has been noted, the preacher's experience of living the Christian life, and of being in relationship with God-in-Christ, is a highly significant element in the preaching task and, indeed, a major resource for it. How can these two aspects of the calling, which would appear to be in tension with each other, be reconciled?

A shared discipleship

The call to preach needs to be placed firmly in the context of a shared discipleship. The most important thing about any preacher is *not* the fact of being a preacher, it is that he or she is a human being called to follow Christ. Like others in the congregation she is called to love and serve God and neighbour. Like others in the congregation he is in need of grace and mercy from God at all times. Preachers have a shared Christian identity with those to whom they preach or, to put it another way, they have all undergone the same baptism. The great Sri Lankan Christian Daniel T. Niles (1908–70) once defined evangelism as 'one beggar telling another beggar where to find bread'. It could stand as a very fine characterization of preaching too! It reminds us that people do not become preachers because they are superior to others morally, intellectually, spiritually or in any other way; they become preachers simply because God has called them to such a huge and entirely undeserved responsibility.

Shared gifts

It is also imperative that the preacher remembers that a call to preach, great and glorious privilege though it may be, is only one gift and calling among the many that are distributed throughout God's people. The New Testament letters contain no fewer than four lists of such gifts and callings, which help to put things into their proper perspective. They are sufficiently important to warrant some time being spent on them.

The first two lists are found in 1 Corinthians 12.4–31, where the apostle Paul writes about spiritual gifts within the congregation. We can work out from the tone of his writing that there had been some controversy within the Corinthian church about such matters, not least concerning which gifts should be regarded as the most important. Paul begins by telling them that there are various gifts, but they all come from the same source, God's Spirit, and that while there are a variety of services to be performed and activities to be undertaken, 'it is the same God who activates all of them in everyone'. He then lists a number of different gifts, including wisdom, knowledge, faith, prophecy, healing and tongues – preaching is certainly in there somewhere! His conclusion is that all of these come from the Spirit, 'who allots to each one individually just as the Spirit chooses'. Paul goes on to draw an analogy, at some length, with the way in which the various parts of the body need one another in order for the whole body to function properly, and draws the conclusion that every part of the body has to be honoured equally. He sums up this part of his thinking on the subject by telling the Corinthians that they are, together, the body of Christ and, as individuals, members of it. Then he immediately creates another list! This time it is of office-holders who exercise certain kinds of ministry: apostles, prophets, teachers, healers and so on. Paul asks the rhetorical question whether in terms of what they are called to do, these are all the same (obviously they are not), and his point is clear: their callings are different from one another, but each and every one of them is honourable and needed within the life of the Church.

The third of Paul's lists, slightly different in content, and rather shorter than the two already examined (though much the same in intention), is found in Romans 12.3–8. He begins by telling his readers that they ought not to have too high an opinion of themselves! Rather, he says, they should assess themselves according to the measure of their faith. Again, significantly, he uses the analogy of all believers being members of the one body ('we are members of one another', he adds) yet each possessing their own gifts from God. This time round the list includes prophecy, ministry, teaching, exhortation, giving and leading. Preaching is in there too.

The final list is to be found in Ephesians 4.4–13. This may

56

or may not be from Paul's pen (many biblical scholars think Paul did not write Ephesians), but it makes essentially the same point. It speaks of a common calling for all Christian people, as expressed by the well-known phrase, 'one, Lord, one faith, one baptism'. It then refers to the ministries of apostles, prophets, evangelists, pastors and teachers, describing them as gifts of the risen Christ to the Church, 'for building up the body of Christ' – these also include preaching.

In all of these lists the key elements are the same and may be summed up in this way: (a) all Christian believers have in common their membership of the body of Christ, which is the Church; (b) the various different ministries that are exercised within the Church are, each and every one of them, gifts (of God, the risen Christ or the Spirit); (c) all these gifts are needed, even equally needed, in order to make up the total ministry of the Church.

It is not, therefore, just a version of modern political correctness that leads us today to value and honour all those who bring their gifts to the life of the Church. Of course, those who undertake particular tasks, roles and ministries may be called to arduous and difficult responsibilities and may, as a result, be treated with greater honour by the Church (though there can be debate about whether this is right!). But in the final reckoning all stand on the same ground as recipients of the gifts of God.

So then, on the basis both of shared discipleship and of shared gifts, the preacher will not reckon herself as being better than others in any way. It is just that the particular calling that has come to this person is to share the life-giving word of God with others; a beggar himself, he points others to where bread may be found. To say this is by no means to diminish the preaching office (though it might prevent some individual preachers from thinking of themselves more highly than they ought to do). The preaching office as such is a major responsibility. To permit anyone who fancies doing so to get up into the pulpit on a Sunday morning and preach would be a grave misunderstanding of the egalitarianism of those New Testament passages we have been exploring. All Christians have a common calling *as disciples*. Over and above that, people have a calling from God to exercise particular gifts and ministries. All of those gifts are needed and we cannot, in the light of the New Testament, say that one is intrinsically better than, or superior to, another. But they are still *different* from one another. For this reason, as well as for some practical ones, most Christian traditions jealously guard their pulpits and do not permit just anyone to preach. However, what the Church looks for when someone is being examined and tested as a candidate for the role of preacher is not that they are superior to others in some way, but that they have a genuine call from God to this office and work. In the light of these things, what can be said about the way in which the preacher's experience as a Christian disciple informs and resources her preaching ministry?

The shared need

If D. T. Niles's celebrated saying about evangelism may be applied to preaching and preachers, as surely it can and must be, then good preaching must necessarily be done in a spirit of considerable humility – and the actual manner in which it is done needs to convey this.

For most Christians, preachers included, reflection on their Christian experience will reveal need rather than attainment, hope rather than achievement and aspiration rather than success. We know, at the very least, that any progress we may ever have made in following Jesus has usually been slow, often difficult and sometimes painful. We will not parade our spiritual triumphs before the congregation because there aren't very many of them anyway and those that exist won't take much time to recount! Yet, because such things are true, we will want to tell the stories of when and how God's grace has taken hold of us, enabling us to be and to do far better than we ever thought we could. Since such stories are always about God's action in our lives it is possible to tell them in ways that encourage and build up our hearers without ever glorifying us.

The unknown personal story

One way in which this can be done, is by telling the story as if it was about someone else. Indeed, to avoid any danger that the story might end up sounding like boasting, perhaps this is how it should always be done. If we have any doubts about the propriety of slightly tampering with the facts in this way, we might be encouraged by how in 2 Corinthians 12.2 the apostle Paul does precisely this. He begins, 'I know someone who . . . ' but he is undoubtedly referring to himself, and as the passage continues he more or less gives up the attempt to disguise the fact. We, then, have liberty to do the same, though perhaps we should learn to do it rather more successfully! So, instead of saying, 'I have discovered that when I am faithful and regular in prayer I am better able to cope with some of the crises that life throws at me', the preacher might simply say, 'Someone was telling me recently about her discovery that when she is faithful and regular in prayer she copes better with some of the crises that life throws at her.' Such a preacher might go on to add, 'Has that been your experience, or mine? Or have we never got round to trying it?' This brings the congregation into the story on the basis of shared need and aspiration. It does not set the preacher apart as an authority on prayer who is telling other people how to behave in order to be better Christians. Rather, it offers what in the end is God's gracious invitation to discover how being faithful in prayer changes for the better the way in which a disciple deals with the problems of life.

However, there is no reason why, from time to time, a

preacher should not be fairly direct about personal experience when it is appropriate to be so. Every effort ought to be made to ensure that such occasions are neither boastful on the part of the preacher nor embarrassing to those who hear. Again, for the most part, such material will spring from need rather than success. Its aim is always to glorify God, not the preacher. One preacher, a nationally known figure, who held very high office in his denomination, began his sermon to a large congregation one Sunday evening in a northern industrial town somewhat along these lines: 'We have had major problems with one of our children. He has been in all kinds of serious trouble with the law and in other ways, and has caused us real grief. We have asked ourselves where we went wrong as parents, what we have done to deserve it and where God has been in this experience.' The proverbial pin could certainly have been heard to drop. The preacher went on to explore, to great effect, the good news about God who, in Christ, loves us to the uttermost and never gives up on us whatever bad and distressing things we have done. The preacher had no need to begin in that way; the congregation had no knowledge of his personal circumstances and the story could have been left untold. The telling of it, quite briefly and in a manner entirely devoid of self-pity, moved the hearers deeply, and it was God who was glorified on that occasion. What mattered was the preacher's ability to take that very personal set of circumstances and then use it to illustrate something that is at the heart of the gospel – God's unconditional love for human beings.

The preacher's use of personal experience in this way also, of course, resonated with the situation of many in the congregation. There were almost certainly some present who had been through a similar experience and others who were aware of family members or friends who had done so. Even those without children had no difficulty in imagining what the preacher was talking about and in making connections with events in their own lives. This illustrates the great strength of using personal experience in preaching: it enables people to recognize that the things spoken about concern human life as it is actually lived. God is involved in the things that happen to us, good and bad alike.

The known personal story

The preacher on the occasion just discussed was a visitor who need not have shared such personal experience with the congregation, but chose to do so. Most preachers are visitors only on rare occasions. Depending on the way the denomination to which we belong is organized, most preachers end up preaching on a regular basis to the same congregation or group of congregations, and almost certainly live locally to where they preach. In that situation their personal circumstances, at least in outline, may very well be known to those to whom they preach. Matters of personal relationships, such as whether the preacher is single, married, widowed or divorced, or has children or perhaps elderly relatives to care for, will be part of people's mental picture of the person who is standing in front of them and preaching the gospel. There will also be some awareness of the preacher's hobbies, interests and leisure-time activities and of any organizations, campaigns or movements to which the preacher belongs. Preachers who are by nature reserved or shy (and God certainly calls such people to preach) can occasionally find this a touch hard to bear, but there is no avoiding it and, in the end, it has to be reckoned with as part of the cost of the calling.

The plain fact is that congregations know, and need to know, that the person who is sharing the gospel with them is like them, a real human being who is affected by the things that affect them and whose Christian faith has to be lived out as theirs has, in situations that often challenge and test it. It may seem paradoxical, but there are occasions when those experiences that have been negative for the preacher, and that might therefore at first sight appear to work against his or her effectiveness in communicating the good news, can have just the opposite effect. This is amazing good news for the preacher – there are times when God both can and does speak through our lives even though, as we see it, this could not possibly happen! Perhaps we ought not to find this as surprising as we often do. After all, the apostle Paul does say that the treasure of the gospel has been given to the world in 'clay jars', precisely in order that people may see how the power of the gospel comes from God and not from the frail human beings who are entrusted with communicating it (2 Corinthians 4.7).

Take, as an example, the not uncommon situation where a preacher has gone through a marriage breakdown followed by divorce. Except in some very conservative Christian circles divorce has now lost most of the stigma that was once attached to it. Yet there is still a residual feeling that to have been involved in a marriage that ended in that way represents failure by the parties involved. Even when, as is sometimes the case, the divorce was wholly right, even life-enhancing, because it represented the formal end of a relationship that had become exploitative or abusive, there is likely to be some guilt and a sense of failure, certainly for a sensitive Christian. This is because the high ideals with which that Christian marriage began have not, for whatever reason, been brought to fruition. It would never be helpful, or right, for the preacher to refer to unhappy experiences of this sort in a self-justifying way; the sermon must never, ever be used to try and get the congregation to take the preacher's side whether on a personal issue or any other. And it is always prudent to take time to allow raw emotions to settle before anything is said about the situation that gave rise to them. But if that can be done it could be a positive experience for a preacher to give testimony to the way in which being a Christian helped in finding new purpose in life and new hope for the future following such a major personal trauma. Those in the congregation who have experienced similar ordeals of their own will be reassured about the relevance of Christian faith to their own lives. Others will be able to make an imaginative leap into their own circumstances and come to the same conclusion.

On occasion the congregation's knowledge of a preacher's personal circumstances can set up an entirely unintended barrier to the gospel message being heard from that person. An obvious example is where a preacher is also an active member of a political party or prominently engaged in publicly campaigning about particular issues. There may be those in the congregation who are of the opposite political persuasion or who take a contrary view on the issues in question. They may well filter what they hear from the preacher through that particular lens and, as a result, level the accusation that what they are hearing is 'politics in the pulpit'. Dealing with this allegation will not be easy, not least because a politically committed preacher might want to claim that his or her views emerge from a proper understanding of what the gospel is and entails. There is, after all, nothing much wrong with having politics in the pulpit provided what is on offer arises out of an authentic understanding of how the Christian faith affects the way society is organized. If the Church is serious about a desire to see Christian believers active and committed in the political sphere (as it ought to be), congregations should welcome preachers being involved in this way. In their turn, individual preachers might well want to claim that their political and other commitments are a proper working out of their Christian faith. This, surely, is laudable. Problems only arise if it seems that a particular political programme comes first on the preacher's agenda and the gospel is then being twisted in order to support it. Nevertheless, the preacher needs to be aware of how his or her involvement in such things might appear to others and try to ensure that it does not get in the way of God's word being heard.

Religious experience

What has been considered so far relates to the way in which preachers might use their experience of God's love and presence in the business of working out discipleship in everyday life. There is also the question of what is sometimes called 'religious experience', which has historically been valued and stressed more by some Christian traditions than by others. The preacher may, for instance, have a strong conversion experience as part of his or her individual history. The story of the point at which Jesus became real and alive in someone's experience will rightly be important to that person. It is undoubtedly good news, the best news there could be, and it seems not only natural to want to share it but imperative that it be shared. It could be that the call to preach itself sprang from that desire. This is fine as a motivation for preaching. To preach in such a way that Jesus becomes alive and real for our hearers ought to be in some sense the aim of all preaching. At the same time, we need to remember that this may not come about for other people in exactly the same way that it happened for us. If the story is told too often it will lose its impact and its predictability will bore people, but we should not, in any case, assume that God deals with everyone in an identical way. Those who have been through a religious experience that has, quite literally, changed their lives often want everybody else to share in something that has done so much for them and is a source of wonder and joy. There is nothing wrong with that ambition, but it needs to be remembered that God has many ways of changing people's lives. The way in which God comes to another person will not be the same as the way God has come to us. As Samuel Chadwick, a well-known preacher of the nineteenth century, put it, 'God has a secret stairway into every soul.' It is entirely right to covet an authentic experience of God's presence for those to whom we preach, but it is simply inappropriate to assume that such an experience must necessarily follow the pattern it followed for us. We need to affirm the authenticity of what others experience.

Members of the congregation are bound together by a common calling to follow Christ, but they may have little else in common – conceivably, nothing at all! Each of us is a unique individual, and we bring with us our genetic inheritance, upbringing and knowledge of life. We come with differing perceptions of all manner of things and respond in our own personal way to what we are offered by way of information, argument and vision. This is true of specifically religious experience as well. Indeed, in the case of religious experience there is the additional factor that if we have grown up in a particular Christian tradition the manner in which we respond to certain sorts of experience, and the language in which we describe it, will be shaped by that tradition. It is, for example, unlikely that a Baptist or a Methodist will claim to have experienced a vision of the Virgin Mary, though those from some other traditions might well do so. Preachers need to be aware that their own religious experiences, including conversion stories, may be heard and received differently by other people and to be sensitive to that fact in the way they preach.

Drawing others in

The preacher uses Christian experience as a way of affirming the credibility of the gospel in daily existence. It attests the value and authenticity of faith in the business of becoming the people God wants us to be. It is an important resource for preaching. But precisely because it is very personal, it can never be an indisputable way of proving that what is being said is true. It is always an invitation to people to see things from a particular perspective and to discover for themselves how God might be active in their own circumstances. The language the preacher uses is always important, but never more so than here. In Chapter 2 it was suggested that every sermon might have as its aim, 'To speak of things in a way that makes it possible for us to meet with God.' The choice of pronoun in that phrase was quite deliberate: it does not say, 'To speak of things in a way that makes it possible for *them* to meet with God.' This is because, as has already been said, the preacher is the first hearer of his or her own sermon; in Bengel's terms the preacher has already applied the text to him/herself. The preacher is included among those who must hear the word of God this morning. It is very important that we preach in a way that enables members of the congregation to sense this in order to appreciate that the preacher is engaged in the same spiritual quest as themselves. Any sermon will use a whole range of pronouns (I, you, we, they, etc.), depending on context, not least to achieve variety and avoid monotony. Where there is a choice, as there often is, the preacher's default pronouns will usually be 'we' and 'us'.

This is what makes sermons inclusive and draws others in. 'What do *Christians* do when God seems far away?' is perfectly all right, but it is a bit detached and can sound as though the preacher is discussing an interesting theoretical question that may, or may not, have anything much to do with those who are present. 'What do *you* do when God seems far away?' is certainly direct and personal, but somewhat fierce and can raise the spectre of the preacher as an expert who is about to give good advice to the non-experts in the congregation. 'What do *I* do when God seems far away?' is impossibly self-regarding and rather invites the response, 'How should I know and why should I care?' 'What do *we* do when God seems far away?' includes people and draws them in. Here is a preacher who has gone through that experience, knows that other people go through it as well and is, presumably, only asking the question because he or she has at least an inkling of a possible answer. This might be worth listening to, might it not? One beggar is telling other beggars where to find bread. If there are fortunate souls present for whom God never does seem far away they will no doubt be charitable enough to continue listening anyway!

An author's testimony

Authors of books like this one customarily maintain a reasonable degree of detachment in their writing style. They almost never refer to themselves in the first person singular and where the readers are addressed directly 'you' is often used. I have found it quite impossible, and undesirable, to attempt that degree of distance between myself and the readers of this book. The reason for that is straightforward enough: as it says in the Introduction, I have been preaching for over 40 years and I am deeply committed to it. This book is for fellow preachers, or at least for would-be fellow preachers. I am therefore writing for sisters and brothers who are, or hope to become, my colleagues in this great calling, though we may never meet. We, author and readers, have this in common and it makes a difference. I am not writing as an expert who has all the answers, nor as someone who is offering instruction. Rather, this book invites fellow preachers to reflect with me on some of the questions that gather round the whole enterprise. Although I hope to persuade readers of the value of the various perspectives I offer, I trust I have left room for people to come to conclusions that differ from mine. But, quite simply, when writing for fellow preachers about the calling we share, about which I feel passionately, 'we' has often been my default pronoun too – as you may have noticed! I am suggesting that in this regard preachers stand in the same relationship to their congregations as I do to my readers. We share a common calling, which is to be hearers of the word of God and disciples of Christ. As preachers we listen before we speak.

6

The Preacher's Heritage

The preacher's experience as a Christian believer contributes in significant ways both to what is said in preaching and to how it is said. However, it is never the whole of the story. To the congregation preaching may appear to be a highly individual, even a solitary, activity. On Sunday mornings the preacher arrives with a ready-prepared message on which he or she has laboured during the preceding week, the contents of which are a mystery until it is delivered. There is, of course, a degree of truth in this picture; nothing can take away the preacher's responsibility to spend the necessary time wrestling prayerfully with the biblical text and the issues it raises in order to hear the message God wants to communicate. Yet it is not the whole story. As has been seen, the preacher's message, which is essentially an invitation to faith, comes in the context of the calling to committed discipleship. This is a common calling, shared by both preacher and congregation. The person who preaches is a member of the community of faith, the body of Christ, the Church. It is the Church that tests a person's call and authorizes the exercise of the preaching ministry. The preaching is not done into a vacuum, but within the context of the Church's life. All these things mean that the preacher brings to the act of preaching all the baggage of what it means to belong to, indeed to be an authorized spokesperson for, such a venerable institution. The Church today is the heir to over two thousand years of its own history. History is sometimes thought of as just being concerned with what happened in the past, but this is a rather naive view. To some extent we are formed and shaped by that past, even when we consciously choose to reject it. This is particularly true of the history of the Church, where the past has given birth to particular ways of understanding and interpreting both what Christians believe and how they behave. This 'Christian Tradition' (which is what we are essentially dealing with here) is a living thing and no preacher can, or should, be unaware of it or try to ignore it. This is both a challenge and a resource for the preacher.

Tradition

We belong to, and are called to be preachers of, a faith that has been believed in by countless millions of people for over two thousand years. It is a simple fact that were it not for the way in which past generations of Christians believed, taught and preached the faith, there would be no Church today. Christianity would be that sad thing, a dead religion, to be read about in books but of interest only to historians. The fact that it isn't is due, humanly speaking, to Christians having taken seriously the command to go into all the world and make disciples (Matthew 28.19–21).

But there is more to it than this. In each generation, as they have believed afresh, Christians have not only lived out their faith and taught it, they have also reflected on its meaning. They have done this not just in theological writings, but in hymns and prayers, poetry and art, music and film. It is quite likely, for example, that in a balanced act of worship, those who participate will use material from several different centuries. This is one of the ways in which we enter into the lived experience of other believers who have gone before us. The writer on spirituality A. M. Allchin has called this 'the ecumenism of time'. This is the 'tradition' of the Church and it is a significant, if sometimes difficult, part of our inheritance. Some things, judged to have passed the test of time, have entered into the fabric of the Church's life and being, have become part of the way in which the Church understands not only herself, but also the message she is charged to proclaim in her preaching.

Good or bad?

It is not immediately obvious to everyone today that this should be regarded as a good thing. Tradition is often, perhaps increasingly, seen in our society as limiting and constraining, something that prevents us from moving forward. Doing something in a particular way just because that is how it has always been done is no longer thought of as a valid option; most things have to be justified in terms of their contemporary relevance. This is an important viewpoint, though not perhaps the whole truth. It is well illustrated by a story from the Jesuit Anthony de Mello, in which he tells of an ashram community where, because the community cat distracted the worshippers during evening service, the community leader ordered that it should be tied up during the service hour. In due course the leader died, but the cat continued to be tied up. In due course the cat died and so another cat was brought to the ashram in order that *it* could be tied up during evening service. Centuries later, scholars wrote learned treatises on the liturgical significance of tying up a cat when worship is performed. The point is clear enough: tradition, however venerable, needs constant re-examination to ensure that it has continuing validity and usefulness in the life of the Church. Otherwise it can lead to curious things happening and the reasons for them may be misunderstood and misrepresented. From time to time in its long history the Church (at least in what we call western Christendom – the Orthodox churches of the East see tradition very differently) has found it necessary to sweep away those traditions that it judged to have become useless, burdensome or positively misleading. When it has occurred that has usually been a painful and divisive process. Yet, when all is said and done, a version of Christian faith that attempted to divest itself of all tradition would scarcely be recognizable as Christianity at all. The Christian faith is not something that we invent but something we receive as a gift.

The great tradition

We have already explored the notion that the Bible is the primary resource and authority for the Church's life and therefore for preaching because it is a book of witnesses to what God has done in human history and, above all, in Jesus Christ. The Church's tradition is, essentially, the cumulative way in which Christians have worked out what Scripture means for human living. The author of the fourth Gospel records Jesus telling his disciples shortly before his death that the Holy Spirit would teach them everything (John 14.26). Some Christian traditions (most notably the Roman Catholic one) interpret this to mean that the Holy Spirit guides the Church to discover and then express in its teachings the whole of God's truth. This is neatly expressed in a verse by Cardinal John Henry Newman (1801–90):

> And I hold in veneration,
> For the love of Him alone,
> Holy Church as his creation,
> And her teachings as His own.

From this perspective, the tradition of the Church is in itself a source of authoritative truth. Other Christians have considerable difficulty with this position and would argue that tradition can never be a primary resource because only Scripture is the primary witness to God's truth. Tradition grows out of, and is therefore dependent on, the Scriptures themselves. This is not the place to attempt to resolve this issue! However, it may be noted that if, as has already been said, the Church's tradition is in essence the cumulative way in which Christians have worked out what Scripture means for human living, most preachers do not need, in practice, to be greatly troubled by it. It would be absurd not to recognize that the promised Holy Spirit has been at work down two thousand years of Christian history, to guide the Church into a fuller appreciation of what the Scriptures say and mean. It is in this sense that tradition is a resource for the preacher.

To take a relatively straightforward example: nowhere in the Bible is polygamy forbidden and, indeed, the Old Testament contains numerous examples of it. It appears, for the most part, to have been a practical arrangement to ensure that the weak and vulnerable were cared for by being part of a household. We cannot be quite sure what happened among the early Christians if a new convert proved to have more than one marriage partner, though it is likely that those relationships were allowed to continue. However, as time went on, and in very different social circumstances, Christians came to see that there could be other ways of caring for widows than by polygamous marriage (Acts 6.1). Wherever marriage or a marriage-related topic is discussed in the New Testament, it is in ways that presuppose that marriage is understood as the personal relationship between one man and one woman (e.g. Ephesians 5.25–33). Guided by the Holy Spirit, we may think, the Church gradually came to the conclusion that polygamy was incompatible with the ideals of Christian marriage. This is now the Church's pretty well universal tradition. Of course, all traditions are open to challenge and from time to time even this one has been so challenged (there are some African churches that do permit polygamy and there is a tiny Christian polygamist movement even in the West), but overwhelmingly the Christian tradition has taken the view that monogamy is the state of life that best expresses the New Testament's teaching on marriage. This is not up for significant discussion in any mainstream Christian denomination, nor ever likely to be. What this means for the preacher is that it would not be acceptable or permissible to preach a sermon advocating polygamy on the grounds that the Scriptures do not forbid it. If this example seems somewhat far-fetched (who, after all, would want to preach such a message?) that is in itself a reminder of how the Church's tradition has become part of the unquestioned backcloth of our thinking. It also tells us that this 'living tradition' within which we preach imposes some disciplines and constraints upon those who preach.

Other instances are much less clear-cut. Christians often have to wrestle hard with the tradition they have inherited and real questions arise about whether it still serves the cause of the gospel, or whether it now distorts the real meaning of the Bible. An obvious contemporary example (though a somewhat complicated one) is the role of women in the leadership of the churches. Should a woman be permitted to preach or speak in church or be ordained? For some Christians this is a simple biblical issue; they judge that the New Testament explicitly forbids putting women in such leadership positions. Others genuinely reach the opposite conclusion from a careful reading of the Scriptures, arguing that such passages must be understood against the social context in which they were written, which is not the same as ours. But the arguments about what the Bible says (and what it means and intends by what it says) are only part of this picture. There can be no serious dispute that the Church's mainstream tradition does not include ordaining women (it is less clear about allowing women who are not ordained to preach). So is that tradition one of God's gifts to the Church, the way in which the Scriptures must be understood and lived out for all time? Or is it merely a human tradition that can be re-evaluated, or even set aside, in the very changed circumstances in which the Church now operates? Or can the ordination of women perhaps be seen as an outstanding example of the 'more light' that the Puritan John Robinson famously said the Lord had ready to break forth from his holy word? Such questions are not easily answered and there is, as always, passion on both sides. Fortunately, perhaps, the preacher is not, in one sense, required to answer questions like this, but does need to be aware of how this kind of tradition is being handled in the denomination to which he or she belongs. Because it is a living tradition in which we stand there is a constant requirement to be in dialogue with it and to be aware that, as with views about the Bible, Christians do not always see things in the same way.

The Church's tradition, then, constitutes a resource for understanding how the gospel can be preached and lived out, but it is a resource that the preacher will handle with care because it requires constant testing against those writings that witness to the original events.

Thus far we have been considering tradition in the sense of those things that belong to the life of the whole Christian Church, irrespective of denomination. But there are also 'lesser' traditions that belong only to particular denominations. These may involve a particular way of understanding what Christians believe – an *emphasis* perhaps. More likely, they are about 'the way we do things'. If we have grown up in a particular denomination and remained within it we may scarcely recognize such things as a 'tradition' in which we stand; we tend to assume that everybody else does it that way (or thinks in that manner) as well! It is only when we become involved in activities that include Christians from traditions other than our own that we come to realize this is simply not true. These lesser traditions are often passionately defended, especially by those who have known nothing else, but with rare exceptions they do not carry any intrinsic authority. In an ecumenical age when we more often encounter churches other than the one to which we belong, and may share worship on a reasonably frequent basis, they may be thought of as the 'treasures' that a denomination brings to the ecumenical pot, though one person's treasure can be another person's dross. The preacher needs to learn something of the ethos that these traditions create in order to exercise a preaching ministry well, but they should not be regarded as definitive, binding or constraining.

History

The Church can decide to change, reform or discard a traditional way of understanding or acting, however painful it may be to do so. But she cannot change her history; she is stuck with it (though there is a constant process of reinterpreting it). The history of the Church as an institution contains many dark and shameful episodes. Christians have frequently behaved badly, not just to people of other faiths and none, but also to each other; they sometimes still do. This is another stick the non-believer can sometimes use to beat the Church, often with justification.

Inspiration and warnings

For the preacher, the history of the Church offers both inspiration and warnings. It is sometimes said that the reason we need to study history is in order not to repeat its mistakes and that is, or ought to be, true. At one level, learning a little of the history of the Church is a powerful corrective to the naivety that sometimes afflicts those who preach! It is church history that stops us from saying things like, 'If everybody became a Christian there wouldn't be any more wars.' It would hardly be possible to maintain that opinion in the face of the frequency with which Christians have waged war on one another. Acknowledging the sins of the Church's past is as essential to the preacher as acknowledging the dark places within our own being. Preaching out of the Church's collective experience of living the gospel ought to be as clear-eyed and realistic as preaching out of our personal Christian experience.

At another level, recognition of the shadow side of the Church's past is a healthy corrective to the assumption that Christian preachers are apt to make, somewhat unthinkingly, that people of faith and prayer usually get things right, whereas secular people do not. In 2007 the British churches, along with many other people, celebrated the 200th anniversary of the passing of the parliamentary Bill that abolished the slave trade in the British colonies. The acknowledged leader of the campaign to bring this about was William Wilberforce (1759–1833), and it is clear that his Christian faith was the driving force behind his lengthy struggle. Yet it is also true that many of those who engaged in the slave trade were themselves Christians and that churches and Christian missionary organizations actually owned slaves. Astonishing as it may seem to us today, they quite often attempted to justify it on the grounds of what they read in the Bible. These two things need to be held in tension with one another.

One of the values for preachers in acquiring this kind of historical perspective is that it enables us to examine the Church's involvement in the issues of today with more critical detachment than we might otherwise muster. When we recognize how Christians of previous generations sometimes failed to see the implications of the gospel for their times we may be better equipped to ask: What attitudes and actions that Christians espouse today will be regarded by future generations with as much astonishment as we now view Christian involvement in the slave trade? We cannot ever fully know the answer to that question, but the act of asking it can save preachers, and therefore the Church, from complacency.

But if the history of the Church contains warnings that the preacher will do well to heed, it also shows how, when the faith is lived out with integrity, it makes a real difference in the lives of individuals and communities. The preacher needs to know and use some of those stories, because if, as has been said, the Christian story is about God's dealings with people, then the stories of the people with whom God deals are important. Little is known about some of those who are celebrated by the Church as 'saints', and tales about others are evidently legendary. But plenty of good things remain, and a good dictionary of the saints provides the preacher with many inspiring stories of courage and wisdom in spreading and living the gospel. That is only a starting-point, for most of the men and women whose lives have best exemplified what it is to be a Christian have never been through any formal process of canonization, either because they belonged to a denomination that has no formal procedures for such a thing, or for some other reason. Their stories, which we find in biographies and newspaper and magazine articles as well as church history books, are equally part of the history of the Church and therefore part of the precious heritage with which the preacher works.

One slightly curious tendency that preachers sometimes show is to think that church history began when their own particular denomination came into being, whether that was by process of reformation or separation or in some other way. Now the history of a denomination is important, and cherishing that history may be a key ingredient in upholding the denomination's sense of identity. But to think and preach as if Christian history began in the sixteenth or eighteenth or any other century is quite wrong. The walls of our separation do not reach up to heaven, as is often rightly said. Those whose discipleship made a difference to the world in which they lived are gifts of God to the whole Church. Their lives show what can happen when the light of Christ shines through and they point, of course, not to themselves but to Christ. So the grace that was manifested in their lives should be celebrated by all. The preacher who learns how to tell the stories of that grace in action will enlarge the vision of the congregation.

The long-term view

There is another sense in which the history of Christianity (even the history of the Church as an institution) can provide the preacher with encouragement and inspiration. It is, essentially, about the long-term view, which is something every preacher needs to take.

Nobody would deny that Christianity in the western world is in trouble. If a personal reminiscence may be permitted: when I offered for ordained ministry nearly forty years ago, someone said to me, 'I don't know why you're bothering. The Church won't exist by the time you come to retire.' That view has proved somewhat pessimistic, but not entirely without foundation. We are all aware of the statistics of decline and that it has been taking place over many years. Closing church buildings, falling numbers at worship and ageing congregations are a sad fact of life with which Christians in contemporary Britain have to live. There are serious projections that suggest that we may have reached a 'tipping point' and that the Christian Church in Britain could effectively cease to exist well within the lifetime of someone who might be reading this book; our great cathedrals, and other listed buildings being museums for tourists, the rest turned into flats and carpet factories. Nobody who is called to preach at the present time can be unaware that this is the context in which we may be operating in the future. And for all the brave, imaginative and resourceful talk and action about 'new ways of being church' and 'fresh expressions of church' there is little evidence as yet (though it may come) that such bold experiments are producing significant numbers of communities of vibrant and committed Christians. So, to put it at its crudest – why bother? Why should anyone go through all the struggles involved in being formed as a preacher of the Christian gospel if, in a few years time, there is not going to be anybody left to hear the preaching?

If what was said in Chapter 1 (that exploring a call to preach is a faith exploration rather than a job application) is correct we will not be deterred by such gloomy prognostications. It is at this point that some knowledge and understanding of Christian history can be helpful. To put it at its simplest: we have been here before. Well no, that isn't quite true. Never before has the Church been where it is now because history does not simply repeat itself. But we *have* been in places that, for those who were involved, seemed at least as dark and difficult to them as ours do to us.

There are many individual locations that, for a time, were centres of Christian faith and learning, but that for one reason or another had their Christian witness destroyed. As just one example we might take Lindisfarne, or Holy Island, whose monastery was founded by St Aidan around 635 and that became the base for Christian mission in the whole of the north of England. Yet only just over 150 years later, in the famous words of the Anglo-Saxon Chronicle: 'On 8 January of the same year, the ravaging of heathen men destroyed God's church at Lindesfarne.' This, usually taken to describe the first Viking raid on Britain, must surely have seemed to the monks whose mission was based there to be the end of the world or, at least, the end of Christian missionary endeavours. But it was not so. The faith flourished elsewhere and, in Lindisfarne itself, a monastic settlement was re-established in Norman times, only to be suppressed in 1536 under Henry VIII. And today? Lindisfarne continues to attract visitors not just because of its isolation and natural beauty, but because of its tradition of spirituality. All is not lost because the barbarians appeared to have won! Some knowledge of Christian history teaches the preacher this important truth.

What is true for places like Lindisfarne has been true on a

much bigger scale, sometimes for whole countries. The Church has been driven out, or underground, by conquest, oppression or even internal corruption. We may take China, where the story is ongoing, as an example. The Church has existed in China for around 1400 years, though always involving only a tiny minority of the population. After the Chinese Communist Party came to power in 1949 it embarked on a sustained campaign to control, and if possible to eliminate, not just Christianity, but all religion. Many stories of oppression and persecution reached the West, and during this period many people thought that, although some kind of underground Church seemed to have survived, in practical terms Christianity in China was virtually finished. This picture began to change only with the lifting of some restrictions in the 1970s, when a different story began to emerge. The Church had not only survived the persecutions, it had been strengthened and had grown numerically in a significant way. It is notoriously difficult to obtain reliable figures about such things, but the Chinese government's own figures in January 2007 admit to some 25 million Chinese Christians, with a leaked report from the Chinese Public Security Bureau putting the figure at 35 million. Other sources claim there are as many as 80 million Chinese Christians. Whatever the truth about the figures, there is no dispute that Christianity is the fastest growing religion in the country. The early Christian writer Tertullian (c.160–230) famously claimed that 'the blood of the martyrs is the seed of the Church', and history has consistently proved him right. All is not lost even when the Church is in dire trouble. Some knowledge of Christian history teaches the preacher this important truth.

Of course, since history does not simply repeat itself, we cannot draw specific parallels between our own situation and those of other times or places, and it would be foolish to try. What we can do, however, is to learn the lesson that God's promises are kept. When the New Testament records Jesus as saying of the

Church that 'the gates of Hades will not prevail against it' (Matthew 16.18), that is one of the promises that will be kept. The precise form the Church will take in Britain in the future cannot be known to us, but that is not the point. Rather, the point is to have confidence, as preachers, in God's future for Christian faith and, in turn, to engender that confidence in those who listen to our preaching. This is not an excuse for complacency; it is an invitation to take the faith journey seriously.

Christian people who are weary or dispirited and perhaps fearful of the future, or who may be whistling in the dark to keep their spirits up, or even in denial about the difficulties, need to hear the confidence of faith from those who preach to them. If preaching is the announcing of good news then the good news in this context is not that God will keep things as they are but that in whatever shape the future takes God will be faithful.

In turn, those to whom we preach have their part to play in enabling God's future to come about. The faith that they have received, which has been handed on to them, must be handed on to others. If preaching is the occasion when worshippers meet with a living and faithful God that fact alone will serve to strengthen and encourage people to share with others what they have received and value. That is how the faith is spread and the Church grows. That is how all believers enter into their Christian heritage, which does not belong to the preacher alone.

7

Preacher of the Faith

Preachers, as we have seen, bring to their calling, study and reflection on the Bible, their own experience of discipleship, and an awareness that they stand within the long history and tradition of the Church. But what is at the heart of the message the preacher brings? The old adage that a sermon is 'about God and about 20 minutes' might now need some modification in terms of the suggested duration, but not in respect of its subject matter. All serious preaching is about God, what God is like, how God is involved with us and our world and how we are to find and follow God in our daily lives, in our thinking and our behaviour. The preacher must know about these things in order to speak of them. So how does that come about?

Theology

This brings us to the word 'theology'. In the popular mind this is a word that (like the word preaching) carries rather negative connotations. A politician might be heard to say, 'I don't want to discuss the theology of this' – meaning that he or she is not going to consider all the minutiae of an issue. That, of course, is a gross misuse of the term. Even within the Christian community there is some suspicion of theology. It is sometimes thought of as being drily academic, as tending to complicate matters that ought to be kept straightforward, even as destructive of a simple (and therefore enthusiastic) personal faith. None of this is true. The word 'theology' comes from two Greek words and just means, 'the study of God'. The poet Alexander Pope (1688–1744) thought that studying God was a presumptuous thing to do. In his *Essay on Man* he wrote:

Know then thyself, presume not God to scan;
The proper study of Mankind is Man.

We may also recall Karl Barth's question about how we could dare to speak of God at all, knowing that we can never do so without distorting God's truth. His answer, that in the act of calling us into faith God calls us to be witnesses to that faith, remains crucial in understanding the preacher's task. If we ignore Pope's warning, as we must, it is because he was quite wrong to think that studying God is presumptuous. It would certainly be so if doing theology depended entirely on our human capacity to think our own way into an understanding of God and God's ways with the world, but it does not. The basic materials for theological thinking and reflection are already given to the theologian, the preacher and the Christian community, by God. Christianity is, in essence, a revealed faith. It is the story of God's involvement in human life and history, through the people of Israel, through the life, death and resurrection of Jesus Christ and through the history of God's people, the Church. It is not a story that human beings have dreamed up. As has often been remarked, if you wanted to invent a new religion you would not choose to begin with a Galilean carpenter who was killed as a criminal!

Theology is the way in which Christians, and preachers in particular, weave together the various strands of God's story and draw out its implications for the life of faith. We have already met some of what might be called the 'building blocks' for doing theology, in particular Scripture and the Christian tradition.

It is as well to recognize that, despite the word's rather bad press, for the preacher there is no escape from theology. As soon as we open our mouths in the pulpit we make theological statements. Underlying all our preaching, no matter how simple it may be, lie assumptions about what God is like and what God has done. Even what appear at first sight to be simple or commonplace statements such as 'God is love', or 'God is revealed in Jesus Christ', or 'God forgives our sins' are, of course, deeply theological. So too are the things we may say about ourselves and our world, such as 'human beings were created to have a relationship with God', or 'our society needs the healing only God can bring' – these statements too presuppose a particular understanding of God. Theology is faith thinking. This is essential, even though our reasoning faculties, like all other aspects of our nature, are distorted by inadequacy and sin. We have no choice but to apply our reason to our faith, since rationality is one of the marks of humanity. So if we hope we can get along without theology we would be deluding ourselves, it is present every time we preach. The question for the preacher is whether what we are saying is good theology or bad theology. How might we tell?

The gift

As was argued in Chapter 6, the Christian faith is not something we invent for ourselves but something we receive as a gift. This can be seen from very early on, even within the pages of the New Testament itself. When the apostle Paul wrote to the church at Corinth concerning how their communal gatherings and sacramental observances should be conducted, he referred to what he had 'received from the Lord' and had in turn 'handed on' to them (1 Corinthians 11.23). Elsewhere he writes about the Christian message itself as something that people had received (1 Thessalonians 2.13; 1 Corinthians 15.3). Best known of all, perhaps, is the phrase from an otherwise rather obscure New Testament writing that speaks of the Christian faith as something 'once delivered to the saints' (Jude 3).

It is possible to misunderstand the implications of this, and to do so in ways that inhibit creative and life-giving preaching. If the Christian faith is viewed as a neat, self-contained package that God has delivered to human beings complete and entire, then presumably all that is required of the preacher is to repeat it and pass it on without deviation or alteration. This would be to treat Christian faith purely as a body of knowledge, objective and monolithic, something that could be learned almost by rote, and then passed on by repetition. Even to suggest that shows what an absurd idea it is. If Christianity was intended to be that kind of package, God would presumably have given human beings a detailed book of instructions on what to think and believe and how to behave. Humanity has not been given that (for the Bible is a book of witnesses not an instruction manual), but something far more precious. The gift is of Jesus Christ, Son of God, whose life, death and resurrection are the revelation of what God is like and how God is involved with us. In each and every generation the Church, guided by the Holy Spirit, has to work at unpacking the meaning of that revelation for the age in which she is living. The gift has been given once and for all, but what that gift means for us and its implications for human life and society need to be prayerfully discovered. This opens the door to imaginative and life-giving preaching. The preacher is neither a freelance commentator, at liberty to talk about anything that takes his or her fancy, nor a mere cipher whose task is to repeat arid theological formulae. The preacher is something much more interesting and challenging: a person through whom God's gift is made available to others and who helps people to work out for themselves what it means to be a Christian. This process has been taking place since the earliest days of Christianity, and the preacher is part of the great continuum.

Jesus is Lord

It is widely agreed among biblical scholars that the first Christian confession of faith (creed) was: 'Jesus is Lord' (Romans 10.9; 1 Corinthians 12.3; Philippians 2.11). Making that profession of faith set a man or woman apart from others in a world where there were many gods and many to whom the title 'lord' was given. As the apostle Paul put it: 'Indeed, even though there may be so-called gods in heaven or on earth – as in fact there are many gods and many lords – yet for us there is one God, the Father, from whom are all things and for whom we exist, and one Lord, Jesus Christ, through whom are all things and through whom we exist' (1 Corinthians 8.5–6).

But what did it mean to make that profession of faith? What were its implications for someone's relationship with God? Was it still necessary (if you were a Jew) to offer the old animal sacrifices? What impact did it have on civil obedience if you were a Roman citizen or subject? What sort of relationship should those who made this profession of faith have with one another within the believing community? Did making this profession of faith have any implications for someone's attitude towards money and possessions, or family, or slaves? These, and many other questions, crowded in upon those who confessed the lordship of Jesus. In the documents that make up the New Testament we can begin to see how the early Christians began to think about them and wrestle with them or, in other words, to do their theology. Questions like these often lie behind the way in which particular passages in the Gospels are written, but they emerge most obviously in the New Testament letters. A few brief examples can stand for the rest.

The First Letter of John is largely about what it means to claim that because they are under the lordship of Christ Christians now live in light rather than darkness and about how the claim 'God is love' has ramifications for our relationships. The first nine chapters of the Letter to the Romans explore what Christ the Lord has done in opening up a new relationship with God for those who were born as Jews as well as for those who were not. The Letter to the Hebrews is, for the most part, concerned with how Jesus the Lord has fulfilled and surpassed the ways of worshipping that God had previously given through Moses and the Hebrew Scriptures. The Letter to the Colossians sets out the grand vision that the lordship of Christ is over the whole of creation (as, in a different way, does the book of Revelation).

As preachers, we can observe how the New Testament writers continually draw out the implications of God's gift to the world, Jesus Christ, for their own times and reflect that, when we preach, we are essentially doing much the same thing. Only, we have their seminal reflections to draw on, and a further two thousand years of Christian thinking to resource us.

Creeds

How then do we, as believers or preachers, know that our beliefs and views about the implications of saying 'Jesus is Lord' are legitimate or correct (and who decides how you measure legitimacy or correctness)? These are huge and complicated questions that have engaged the minds of many great theologians and philosophers, and still do. The apprentice preacher does not need to know all the ins and outs of them, but does need to have some appreciation of what might be called the boundaries of preaching. After all, when someone becomes a preacher they take on the role of an authorized spokesperson for the Christian faith. Paul described himself as a 'steward of God's mysteries' (1 Corinthians 4.1), and that is true of all preachers. So, on the one hand, preaching is not about giving voice to our own opinions while, on the other hand, it is not about a mechanical repetition of received truths or doctrines. The creativity of preaching lies somewhere between those two things, always remembering that if God has called us to preaching it is, at least in part, because there is some gift or understanding that we possess which will enrich the Church's message (even though we often doubt it!).

The boundaries of preaching (that phrase offers a rather imperfect description of what is meant, but it is hard to think of a better one) are represented by the historic creeds of the Church. Some Christian traditions still include one or more of these in worship on a regular basis, so they may be relatively familiar. Other denominations use them much less regularly in worship, even perhaps not at all. Most mainstream churches have them as part of their official statements about what they believe and stand for. They codify the doctrines of the Christian Church. Quite often, when people are being admitted to the office of a preacher (whether as a lay person or by ordination), they will be asked whether they believe the doctrine of the Christian faith as that particular denomination has received it. The historic creeds are the basis for that doctrine.

There are two historic creeds likely to be familiar to the preacher. One is the Apostles' Creed, so-called because of the legend that it was written by the twelve apostles on the Day of Pentecost, each apostle contributing a clause. The real origins are more complex than that and there are many scholarly theories about them. The second historic creed is usually known as the Nicene Creed. Its origins are also extremely complicated, but it was first adopted at the Council of Nicaea in 325 (hence its most common name) and then in a revised and expanded form at the Council of Constantinople in 381. Two of its phrases were added subsequently, 'God from God' and, with reference to the Holy Spirit, the words 'and the Son' – an addition that split the Church and is still the subject of controversy today.

Before we consider the Nicene Creed as both a resource and a boundary for the preacher, two general points need to be made. In the first place, no creed is intended to be an exhaustive statement of what Christians believe. They are summaries, intended to serve as a yardstick for correct belief. Many scholars think that the earliest creeds were intended to be memorized by new believers so that they could discern whether the preaching they heard was orthodox or not. In the second place, by defining what was judged correct or orthodox, creeds either explicitly or implicitly deny the correctness or orthodoxy of other views. Quite a lot of (sometimes rather unedifying) theological controversies lie behind each of the creeds, and the particular disputes that were taking place at the time largely define what they say, or do not say. The preacher does not need to know about those controversies in any detail, but does need to know that they existed. It is, in any case, useful to be reminded that the Church's understanding of the gospel was thought through (sometimes fought out) not in some academic setting, but in real debate. These were issues that mattered – and they still do!

The Nicene Creed: resource and boundary

The Nicene Creed we use in worship is a translation into English from a Greek original. There are a number of such translations. The one that is used in this discussion was published in 1988 by the English Language Liturgical Commission, an international and ecumenical body charged with the task of producing English-language versions of many different texts intended to be used by all the churches. In practice, some denominations have chosen not to use this version at all, while a good many others have adopted it in a modified form and such modifications vary between the churches.

Believing in one God

We believe in one God,
  the Father, the Almighty,

maker of heaven and earth,
of all that is, seen and unseen.

In this section the Church confesses her faith in the existence
of one supreme deity in whom all things have their origin. It
affirms that there is only one God (this is known as monothe-
ism). Christianity holds this view in common with some other
world faiths such as Judaism and Islam though, quite obviously,
they would define and describe God in ways that sometimes
differ from the ways in which Christians do so. The creed here
describes God as 'Almighty', by which it means 'able to do all
things'. This does not in itself tell us about the things God *chooses* to do. Some of the later clauses of the creed describe God's
choices, but the use of the word 'Father' at this point takes, as
it were, a peep forward. In recent times in some quarters it has
become a controversial way of defining or describing God. This
is partly because it is a masculine word and God is, obviously,
beyond gender. It is also the case that some people have such
bad experiences of abuse from their human fathers that they
cannot use the word with reference to God. The preacher needs
to be sensitive to these things, but the Christian tradition cannot stop calling God Father. It is in the creed because it is one of
the given things about Christian faith. This is the gift that Christians have received and without it the next section of the creed
does not make sense. What the preacher must do is to take care
that in speaking of God's nature as Father the language that is
used is appropriate in helping congregations to understand that
God's fatherhood transcends even the best that human fathers
can offer. Moreover, such language is about a relationship rather
than about gender. And, of course, it is not an exclusive term.
Other images of God (including 'mother', which can be thought
equally difficult) can and should be used alongside it in preaching.

Believing in one Lord, Jesus Christ

> We believe in one Lord, Jesus Christ,
> the only Son of God,
> eternally begotten of the Father,
> God from God, Light from Light,
> true God from true God,
> begotten, not made,
> of one Being with the Father;
> through him all things were made.
> For us and for our salvation
> he came down from heaven,
> was incarnate of the Holy Spirit and the Virgin Mary
> and became truly human.
> For our sake he was crucified under Pontius Pilate;
> he suffered death and was buried.
> On the third day he rose again
> in accordance with the Scriptures;
> he ascended into heaven
> and is seated at the right hand of the Father.
> He will come again in glory to judge the living and the
> dead,
> and his kingdom will have no end.

In this long central section the Church confesses her belief in Jesus Christ, the only Son of God and Saviour of the world. Paradoxically, it might seem as if this part of the creed is somewhat remote from the way we often speak and preach about Jesus. There is no mention here of his earthly ministry, which occupies much space in the Gospels and therefore often provides the basic subject matter for preaching on Sundays. There is no clause that states, for example, 'He healed the sick and taught us how to live in accordance with God's will.' Such an omission might seem strange to us because those are the things that appear to be of most immediate interest to us and our congregations. But this is a reminder to us that the creeds are essentially summaries of what God has done (and is still doing) for the world's salvation. Healing the sick and preaching the good news were demonstrations of what happens when God's reign comes to human lives. They did not in themselves provide a way of salvation, but the death of Jesus on the cross did. In this way the creeds remind preachers to look at the Gospel stories from the perspective of the whole.

There is, of course, far more in this section of the creed than it is possible to unpack, or even allude to, here. The preacher who ponders its contents will note that some common views about Jesus (that he was just a very good human being, for example) are implicitly or explicitly rejected as inadequate. The essential things that this creed says about Jesus are that he shares in the very nature of God, became incarnate as a human being at a particular time and place, was put to death and rose from the dead, that he has dominion over all things, now and in the future, and that all this was and is 'for us and our salvation'. The preacher's task is to find ways of saying these things that make sense to people today.

Believing in the Holy Spirit

> We believe in the Holy Spirit, the Lord, the giver of life,
>   who proceeds from the Father and the Son,
>   who with the Father and the Son is worshipped and glorified,
>   who has spoken through the prophets.
> We believe in one holy catholic and apostolic Church.
> We acknowledge one baptism for the forgiveness of sins.
> We look for the resurrection of the dead,
>   and the life of the world to come. Amen.

The final section of the Nicene Creed is concerned with the person and work of the Holy Spirit and with the Church. The description of the Holy Spirit as having 'spoken through the prophets' asserts the continuity of God's revelation in the Old Testament and the history of Israel with the New Testament and the history of the Church. Implicit rather than explicit is the notion that those who have been claimed by Christ in baptism live out their Christian lives with the help of the Holy Spirit and, as a result, can look forward in hope and confidence to the resurrection of the dead and the life of the world to come.

The idea of God as Trinity (God is Father, Son and Holy Spirit) is strongly present throughout. God has an only Son who is of one being with the Father and the Holy Spirit 'proceeds'; God in Three Persons as the well-known hymn puts it. This is how the Church has known and experienced God's actions in the world and in human history. Consequently, it is absolutely foundational to all Christian thinking and teaching, and therefore to preaching as well. If we feel, as many of us do, that we struggle to grasp the doctrine of the Trinity at anything other than a fairly superficial level, we may quail at the thought that we have to preach on it. In fact we probably don't have to attempt that often, or even at all. The doctrine of the Trinity is to the preacher as water is to a swimmer. It is the environment in which we operate, the backcloth for all our thinking, the way in which the Church understands God.

Faith and doubt

Most churches that use the Nicene Creed in worship use a translation that, like the one above, prefers the corporate 'We believe' rather than the more individual 'I believe' at the beginning of each section. In some liturgies this is emphasized by the giving of an invitation to join in saying the Creed such as, 'Let us confess together the faith of the Church.' This reminds us that creedal statements outline and summarize what is believed by the Church as a whole. It is not, of course, necessarily believed in its entirety by every single member of the Church. Those who are exploring a call to preach may well include themselves among those people who find some Christian doctrines difficult to understand or impossible to accept. Does that act as an automatic disqualification from preaching? Some people would say that it does and that if you cannot honestly say you believe everything that is found in the creeds or taught by the Church, you cannot preach the Christian faith to others. But that, surely, takes much too narrow and rigid a view of the nature of Christian faith. It treats it as primarily a package of intellectual statements to which assent must be given, which it is not. If, however, the Christian faith is essentially about the way in which the story of God-in-Christ is worked out in human life, there is room for some doubt, or at least agnosticism, about some of the details of that and about how it is to be understood. The gospel, we recall, is a gracious *invitation* from God. If Christian doctrine is the working out of the implications of that gospel, then it too must have the character of an invitation, not a demand. Christian doctrine invites believers, including the preacher, to approach life in a particular way and to see things through a particular kind of interpretative lens. Sometimes we may find that this doesn't quite work for us and we cannot, with honesty, say that it does. That needs to be acknowledged and faced. When God calls an individual to preach the gospel, that calling comes to a real person, and real people have doubts and uncertainties as well as sins and weaknesses. In principle, anyway, an inability to believe everything with which we are presented is no more of a barrier to preaching than is the undoubted fact that we are not morally perfect. God understands these things and calls us despite them. For many preachers, perhaps most, living with the tensions that can arise between how one understands one's own personal faith and how one understands what we describe as 'the faith of the Church' is a lifelong process.

Growth and change

It is also about our personal growth in understanding and about the work of the Holy Spirit in our lives. Leslie Weatherhead (1893–1976), a popular preacher in his day, spoke of putting those things about which we are agnostic, or that we find we cannot accept, into a mental box labelled 'awaiting further light'. That is quite good advice for the preacher, provided we remember to take them out of the box from time to time and have another look at them! The preacher, like every believer, is called upon to have humility before the truth. If there is some aspect of Christian faith that we find difficult, one way of approaching it is to assume that if it makes sense to other Christians it may, in God's good time, come to make sense to us as well. By honest and prayerful enquiry and endeavour we will work towards that being so. But we are also required to have honesty and integrity. If we find something impossible to accept we cannot make ourselves believe it, nor should we ever pretend that we do; in pretence lies hypocrisy and so spiritual death.

It is recorded that the great German Moravian Peter Böhler (1712–75) once advised the founder of Methodism, John Wesley (1703–91): 'Preach faith till you have it; and then, because you have it you will preach faith.' That is sage counsel because it encourages us to remember that our personal faith journey is capable of change and development and that God always has new things in store for us. It is also sometimes the case that some aspects of Christian faith do not really register with us, or mean very much to us, until particular life experiences have come our way and changed what we believe to be important. In those cases, too, we need to learn to discern the leading of God's Holy Spirit.

If we reflect on some of those things about which we have doubts and uncertainties, we may discover that they relate to theological theories. It is important to remember that although the Church has defined what orthodox belief is in many significant areas, it has not done so in all. The outstanding instance where this has not happened is in relation to the meaning of the cross. The New Testament is clear enough that Christ's death on the cross has brought humanity forgiveness of sins and the opening up of a new relationship with God. The New Testament uses many different images and analogies to describe and explain this and, reflecting that fact, the Church has never laid down any particular *theory* of the Atonement as being required for correct or orthodox belief (though individual denominations have sometimes, rather unwisely, done so). So there is liberty for the preacher in this respect, and in others too.

The meaning of believing

Above all we must not make the mistake of confusing orthodox theology or doctrine with the actual act of believing. The two are closely connected of course, but it is possible to have some doctrinal doubts and reservations without those things affecting the reality of the faith we profess and preach. This is not always an easy distinction to make because in English we use the word 'belief' in several closely connected but slightly separate senses. 'It is my belief that Britain should leave the European Community' really means, 'In my opinion Britain should leave the European Community.' 'I have great belief in you' means, 'I put my trust in you.' When Christians talk about believing or having faith, they usually mean both these things, but with the emphasis on the latter. So, 'We believe in God' means *both* 'We believe that God exists' *and* 'We trust in God.' It is obviously not possible to trust in God if we don't believe that God exists, but it is possible to trust in God without accepting uncritically all the ways in which God has been described within the Christian tradition.

In such matters we might take our cue from the great statement of faith that is found in 2 Timothy 1.12: 'I know the one in whom I have put my trust, and I am sure that he is able to guard until that day what I have entrusted to him.' This points to the heart of faith, not *what* we believe, but *in whom* we believe. It is Christ who is the object of our faith. What theology and doctrine do is to help us give an account of that faith, why it is reasonable to have it, what having it means and how it coheres with other things. That is why doctrine and theology are such huge resources for the preacher: they help us to 'give an account of the hope that is in us' as the New Testament elsewhere puts it, and that helps to give Christianity credibility in the world in which we live.

There could, of course, be circumstances in which someone's doubts or agnosticism about some major tenets of Christian faith would make it impossible to preach. You cannot invite people to have trust in God if you do not believe that God exists. It would also be very peculiar to want to be a Christian preacher if you thought that Jesus Christ was never raised from the dead (however you might choose to describe the resurrection). In that instance the New Testament itself makes it plain that unless Jesus was so raised Christianity is a sham (1 Corinthians 15). But what about, say, the Nicene Creed's assertion concerning Jesus that, 'He will come again in glory to judge the living and the dead'? It is surely possible to be quite agnostic about what precisely it means to speak of Jesus coming again in glory without compromising one's ability to preach the Christian gospel. And, in relation to the same phrase, it is certainly possible to hold that the judgement to which it refers will be a judgement of mercy and love that will ensure that hell is empty, without ceasing to be an authentic Christian preacher.

Yet even if this is all true, there remains, in theory and sometimes in practice, a tension between the preacher's personal ability to affirm certain Christian orthodoxies and his or her role as an authorized spokesperson for the Church and a teacher of the faith. Congregations have sometimes been known to complain, perhaps with reason, that some preachers are rather too fond of airing their doubts in sermons. Here, preachers need to take their representative role very seriously. On the one hand, many members of a congregation will have their own doubts and uncertainties (though they may be about different things from those that bother the preacher). They will not be helped by a preacher who appears to be full of confident certainties and who speaks as if there could be no possible doubts or reservations about anything at all. Indeed, they might find real difficulty in relating to such a preacher. On the other hand, a preacher who expounds his or her personal doubts certainly does not build up the congregation in faith and can be the target for justifiable criticism.

As a general rule it is sensible to remember that when we are preaching we are in role as a spokesperson for the Church and for the faith of which she is guardian. If there are doctrines that we cannot preach about positively, then we say nothing about them. Because at that moment we are not private individuals charged with delivering our own opinions, we do not have the right to preach in a way that is contrary to that which the Church holds and professes in the creeds. The exploration of doubts and uncertainties, if it is to be done, is more appropriate in house-groups or private conversations where reaction and feedback is possible. But neither should the preacher give the impression of being immune from doubt when that is not the case. Each preacher has to find his or her way of dealing with this sensitively. It would be enough just to say about such a subject: 'This is what the Christian faith teaches us. I personally struggle somewhat with making sense of it, but it is here in our tradition as a challenge.' In matters like these the context in which we are preaching will have a considerable influence on what is said and how it is said.

8

Preaching in Context

In Chapter 4 the question was asked: Why don't denominations appoint a national sermon-writer to produce a weekly sermon that could be distributed to every church and be read to the congregation? The answer given there was that authentic preaching comes from individuals who are called to preach through making use of the developing resources God gives to them. There is another possible answer, an additional one rather than an alternative; people who listen to sermons come from very different contexts, have different needs, hopes, dreams and fears, and need to have sermons that are tailored to their particular circumstances, at least some of the time.

Those exercising a preaching ministry will be helped by having some understanding of the necessary interaction between the preacher's personality and gifts and the congregation's needs and expectations. Expertise in psychology is not required; it is a matter of common sense and spiritual sensitivity!

The 'hit and run' preacher

There are some preachers who, as their preaching ministry begins to develop, find it difficult or even impossible to achieve this. They might preach to a large number of congregations, more or less in turn, and their knowledge both of the corporate life of any one congregation, certainly of the individual people who make it up, will necessarily be limited. In any case, such knowledge and understanding as they do have will be from the outside, as it were. They do not live alongside the people to whom they preach and therefore do not share in the hopes and dreams that can come from sharing the same community life. Those who develop a preaching ministry on a national or international scale have this handicap – if that is what it is – in abundance. Indeed, it is not unknown for busy and tired visiting preachers to, on occasion, mistake the name of the place where they are preaching. These are truly 'hit and run' preachers in the sense that they deliver their message, hope that it does some good to at least some of those present, and then disappear over the horizon. It is usually left to others to deal with the results of the visit, whether those are helpful or unhelpful.

We have deliberately begun our reflection on what it means to preach in particular contexts with this kind of preaching, even though it is highly unlikely that any of the readers of this book will ever find themselves exercising that sort of ministry. The reason is that such preachers usually learn one precious truth about preaching, which actually applies to everybody who preaches and must never be forgotten. It is this: the subject matter of every sermon, no matter where it is delivered or to whom, is what God has done in Christ for every human being. Granted there are real skills to be learned and exercised by the preacher in order to do that well in a context or culture that is not his or her own. But such preachers know that this is the heart of their message because it is the only thing they can talk about that is universally applicable – true in all places, all contexts, all times.

Such preachers are, to a greater or lesser extent, even in this age of globalization, deprived of those things that often act as props for sermons or ways into subjects. They cannot easily begin with references to television programmes or football matches if they are preaching in another country. They cannot convincingly refer to their city council's recent decision on how to deal with homelessness in the city if they are preaching in a village community many miles away. And humour – that much appreciated if often rather dangerous friend to preachers – notoriously travels badly; what is funny in one culture or context can be not only very un-funny in another, it can be open to misunderstanding or even offensive. So what is the preacher left with? Only the big issue of what God has done in Christ for every human being. Both parts of that phrase are important. What God has done in Christ is the story to which the Bible bears witness. That God has done this for every human being, regardless of ethnicity, gender or culture, is lived out in the Church's tradition and history and embodied in the preacher's personal experience. There may, of course, still be important cultural issues to be understood before the preaching can be fully effective, but the story of God in Christ on the one hand, and the universal needs of the human heart on the other, are the two great fixed points around which this preaching must take place.

The apostle Paul preached in many different contexts and, if the evidence of Acts 17.16–31 is to be believed, could take great care to understand the culture he was in so that he could speak to it as effectively as possible. However, when he reminded the congregation at Corinth of what lay at the core of his preaching he wrote: 'I did not come proclaiming the mystery of God to you in lofty words or wisdom. For I decided to know nothing among you except Jesus Christ, and him crucified' (1 Corinthians 2.1b–2). This is true for everyone who preaches. Those whose preaching takes place in much more localized and familiar contexts need to remember it. That said, the context in which the message is delivered is of considerable importance. The sermon that has been carefully prepared for one congregation might be much less effective with another.

The local context

For the most part, those who are called to a preaching ministry expect to carry it out in an environment with which they
are, or with which they will soon become, reasonably familiar.
Sermons will be delivered either to a single congregation or to
a small group of congregations that are linked together in some
way. The preacher may well have been a worshipper in that congregation (or in one of them if there are several involved) and
may even have grown up in that situation. This will probably
not be true (though it may be) if the preaching is undertaken
as part of stipendiary ordained ministry, but where that is the
case the preacher is in a position to enable relationships, and
the pastoral knowledge that goes with them, to develop quite
quickly. There are both strengths and weaknesses in those circumstances, and the preacher needs to be conscious of them.
Indeed, such awareness needs to shape, in quite significant ways,
the kind of preaching that takes place.

When reflecting in Chapter 5 on the preacher's personal
experience of Christian discipleship, it was noted that where
a preacher (and that preacher's strengths and weaknesses as a
human being) may be well known to a worshipping community, this can provide effective entry points for sharing the gospel,
but it can also set up real barriers to effective communication.
This certainly seems to have been the case for Jesus. Luke's Gospel records him as preaching his first sermon in his home syna-
gogue at Nazareth, and how this at first produced a favourable
if slightly astonished reaction from his hearers. However, as it
progressed and its message became decidedly more uncomfort-
able, the approval changed to hostility until, in the end, the situation became quite dangerous (Luke 4.16–30). Jesus knew the
congregation to which he was preaching, and no doubt had very
good reasons for challenging their attitude and understanding
in the way he did. This is the other aspect of the situation: the

congregation's knowledge of the preacher plays its part, but the preacher's awareness of the individual circumstances of members of the congregation is even more important.

The pastoral context

'We really needed to hear that message this morning. I don't know how you knew' is a quite common remark made to visiting preachers as they shake people's hands at the church door after the service. Sometimes the preacher *did* know, because someone else, maybe the local priest or minister, has passed on the information that influenced the message. More often, all the preacher can do is to reflect that it was really God who knew and that the message arose from what 'happened' to be the lectionary reading for the day! But if the local priest or minister had in fact passed on such information to a visiting preacher it is easy to see why. The unpalatable fact is that if we are preaching to a congregation we know well it is sometimes very difficult, even impossible, to deal with particular topics or issues, yet they may need to be dealt with. This may be because we are perceived as being already involved in something that is controversial and the pulpit is never the place to pursue a personal agenda; that would be a severe misuse of our calling. Or it may be because we know that there are people present for whom a particular issue is very personal and very agonizing as they try to work through what it means for them to be a Christian. A sermon is never, ever, to be used as a way of commenting on the attitude, behaviour or situation of an individual; that would be inexcusable.

We recall that one of the dictionary definitions that we explored in Chapter 2 was clearly intended to be negative: 'a long talk in which someone advises other people how they should behave in order to be better people'. While no serious practitioner of the art of preaching ever sets out to write a sermon that does that, it would appear that, regrettably, that is sometimes how sermons come across to those who hear them. One of the main reasons for this is the almost inevitable tendency for sermons to contain sweeping and generalized statements. If they are not nuanced or qualified they sound condemnatory and dismissive – and there will be those among the hearers who will feel, with some justice, that they, their needs and their struggles, have been condemned and dismissed. That does not help anyone to grow in the grace of God or to lead a better Christian life.

Take, as a (deliberately) controversial example, the area of human sexuality. Some denominations have taken a clear stance on homosexuality in particular, either 'conservative' or 'liberal' – to use those unfortunate and misleading terms. Most churches are in turmoil and tension about the issues. The preacher will almost certainly have his or her own views about such matters, and those views may, or may not, be the same as the official denominational line, if there is one. What good would be achieved by a preacher saying, in the course of a sermon, 'God loves gay people and we should bless their relationships in church'? Granted, there might be some present who would feel affirmed, either personally or on behalf of family members, by such a statement, but there would be others for whom it would be a source of offence and outrage. Equally, what good would it do for the preacher to say, 'God loves gay people but hates what they do and they must stop'? There would be some present who would doubtless nod their heads in firm agreement, but others would be deeply hurt and wounded either on their own behalf or that of others. And where, in either of those statements, is the gracious invitation that is at the heart of preaching the gospel?

This is, admittedly, a controversial example and a hard case. There are times when controversy cannot be avoided. But the question 'What good would it do to say this?' can be a useful litmus test to determine which topics should or should not be dealt with in sermons in public worship. Certainly there are issues that *do* need to be tackled and, as we have seen, the preacher who comes from outside the situation may, paradoxically, be best placed to do so. But others simply do not need to be preached about. They are better tackled in personal conversation where there is opportunity for interaction and expression of other perspectives, or perhaps in study groups where the same is true. The preacher's growing knowledge of the people to whom he or she is preaching will provide guidance in this area.

The nature of the congregation

Congregations are, for the most part, much less homogeneous than once they were. This is the case with denominational allegiance. Most churches, certainly the larger ones, include people whose roots are in another denomination. Those who move a considerable distance from their previous homes for job-related reasons or on retirement often shop around for a new church and will join one with which in various respects they feel comfortable, regardless of its denomination. For the preacher this means that some quite important assumptions about the nature of the Christian community and how it operates can no longer be taken for granted. But the issue goes deeper than this.

In Britain at least, the parish system provided a template that, broadly speaking, governed which church people attended, until somewhere around the middle of the twentieth century. The availability of easy transport was a major factor in this. When most people walked to church (or rode in horse-drawn carriages if they were wealthy), they by and large went to the church nearest to where they lived. If they belonged to a denomination with relatively few church buildings, that might have entailed a somewhat longer journey, but the principle still held good. In a large town or city where a number of churches might be within walking distance other factors, such as the style of worship or the quality of the preaching, might persuade people to attend a place of worship a little further away from home, but perhaps not very much further away.

What this meant was that each church hosted a congregation that was fairly representative of the locality in which it was set. The church in a northern industrial town that was surrounded by back-to-back housing would have a congregation largely comprised of industrial workers (though the factory owners often went there as well in order to keep an eye on 'their workers' and sat in a separate pew). A church in a rural village could expect a congregation largely composed of agricultural workers, together with the squire and his relations (who also sat in a separate pew). The congregation of a church in a leafy suburban area might be slightly more mixed, but might be made up of successful business people, senior local government officers and academics (the servants went in the evening). The people who made up each worshipping community would have a great deal in common with each other in terms of their daily experience, their hopes and aspirations and the limitations placed on what they and their children might be expected to achieve in life. They would have comparable incomes and therefore lifestyles and would share a good many assumptions about what was expected of them by others. At one level this enabled a preacher to know what kind of congregation she or he was dealing with, to use appropriate language and illustrations and deal in shared suppositions about life and faith.

This rather generalized picture of how things used to be is a dramatic reminder that they are like this no longer. Churches today are very rarely homogeneous in this kind of way. The exceptions may come from opposite ends of the spectrum: on the one hand, some Urban Priority Areas where, apart from people who are trying to get their first step on the housing ladder, congregations are largely made up of the poor and less well educated and, on the other hand, prosperous suburbs where the affluent and well educated live. But by and large, the world in which the preacher now operates is one in which people readily travel to Sunday worship, sometimes long distances and often to the church in which they grew up even though they left the area long ago. At one level this is quite positive, because most churches now more readily reflect the diversity of God's human creation. But it can make life rather more difficult for the preacher! It means that those who preach cannot easily take for granted that there are many common assumptions or attitudes. Sadly, it can also mean that there is a reduced commitment to the area in which the church is placed because people do not actually live there.

The preacher can, and should, regard all this as a challenge. Forming relationships with people in the congregation, thereby learning what 'makes them tick', what they hope for out of life, what problems they live with and so on, is now important for all who preach and not just for those who have professional pastoral responsibilities within the life of the church. It is through conversations and contact that the preacher discovers those things that will speak to her hearers. This is not simply a question of relevance. Relevance is a somewhat over-used word; when people dismiss something as being irrelevant they often mean no more than that they do not like or understand it. Part of the art of preaching is to help others discover things in the Christian faith that are more relevant than they might ever have imagined, but we do that most effectively when we have begun to understand why the relevance might not be immediately obvious to them.

One of the preaching skills that is most vulnerable to the lack of congregational homogeneity is the use of illustrations. These are quite often economically, socially and culturally limited, though we are sometimes slow to recognize the fact. In part this is because we tend to illustrate from what we ourselves know and experience and often make the unconscious assumption that our hearers are just like us. Well, they may be, but on the other hand they may not. Or, as is more likely, some of them will be and some of them will not. Some things are a matter of simple common sense. To begin an illustration with, 'We know how we feel when our train is very late or cancelled', in a sermon to a village congregation thirty miles from the nearest railway station, is not likely to ring many bells, but to do it with a congregation who mostly have (or had) to commute into the city by train each day would be a different story. Such things are indeed just a matter of common sense, and the point does not need to be laboured.

Other things may be subtler than that. Illustrations from a television soap will resonate with some people but pass others by completely. Those drawn from the latest prize-winning novel will have the same result. And which newspaper do you, the preacher, read? If you read the *Guardian*, references to something that has 'been in the news this week' can reveal the fact that it may not have been in the news this week for those who read the *Sun*, or the other way round. The preacher needs to learn to *vary* the kind of illustrations he uses and to take them from many different and contrasting sources. At the beginning of a preaching ministry this seems like an immense task and we may wonder how it could ever be done. But it is generally the case that, as part of their formation, preachers begin to look at life differently, not quite as preaching-fodder, but as revealing the presence (and sometimes the absence) of the living God. Although this is not a 'how to' book, it would be remiss not to counsel the budding preacher that the age-old advice to keep a scrapbook, notebook or commonplace book, in which things can be jotted down and where cuttings can be pasted in, is very good advice indeed!

The listening context

Most congregations contain some people who know how to listen to a sermon and derive something worthwhile from it and other people who find that more difficult. However, it is one of the great mysteries of church life that some congregations *as a body* are good at listening to sermons and others are terrible at it. There may be individual people present who exhibit the opposite characteristics, but the congregation as a whole falls into one category or the other. This is often commented upon when preachers gather together. There are congregations that appear to be totally unmoved by even the most splendid sermon and their body language tells the story; they simply are not prepared to get involved. Some years ago a Lancashire vicar, on leaving his parish, was reported in the national press as saying that the only way to stimulate any interest among the congregation would be to have a performing elephant in place of the sermon. Fortunately, not many congregations drive their preachers to that kind of despair. Other congregations listen to sermons with rapt attention, even with nods and grunts of agreement (or perhaps slight shakes of the head to indicate disagreement) and the preacher may well find herself engaging in a number of conversations at the church door or over coffee afterwards about what was said. The mystery is that it is usually difficult or even impossible to discern why a particular congregation should fall into one or another of those two categories. If congregations that listen well do so because they have been regularly given preaching that has nourished them (which seems a reasonable proposition), it would seem logical to suppose that the opposite is also true and that unresponsive congregations are created by dull, boring and unchallenging preaching. Perhaps they are, but not always. The evidence suggests that some consistently stimulating preachers have this problem with which to contend, so there is a mystery here! Nevertheless, the preacher should at least try to find ways of awakening interest, though stopping short of employing performing elephants.

Learning how to begin a sermon is rather important. The present writer once heard a sermon (on the Second Sunday of the Easter Season moreover), which began: 'Today I would like us to consider some aspects of the iconoclastic controversy of the ninth century.' It would seem superfluous to point out what was wrong with that. The sad thing is that it was, on the whole, quite a good sermon, largely about how various images of Jesus might help us in our faith today. We might wonder how many of the hearers lasted long enough to discover that. There is no such thing as a good formula for beginning a sermon. Every preacher has to discover for him- or herself how to do it – preferably to discover a number of different ways of doing it. But in general it helps to remember that preaching is direct speech, not a read essay. So, 'Today I would like us to consider . . . ' is not a good way to begin, no matter what comes next. Sometimes a question that arises from the text or the passage on which the sermon is based and that, because it has arisen in the mind of the preacher, has probably also arisen in the minds of many in the congregation, is a good way in. A very effective sermon arose from Romans 8.28, 'We know that all things work together for good for those who love God' when, after reading the text, the preacher's opening words were, 'Do they really? It often doesn't look like that.' The congregation could be seen, visibly, to sit up! They had probably feared a bland ten minutes on everything being for the best in the best of all possible worlds. Instead, they were given a searching exploration of what Paul might have meant by saying such a thing, and whether he was right.

If beginnings are important, so are endings (which is not to say that what comes in between is not important as well!). Many of us suffer from a desire to wrap things up in neat little parcels, to write QED at the close, and to present our hearers with a worked-out and logical argument. Sermons are not meant to be like that and, in any case, most people do not listen like that. If we look at the parables and stories of Jesus we discover that a good many of them could be described as open-ended. The story itself is usually complete, but its meaning is hinted at rather than spelled out, and the hearers left to draw their own conclusions about what it might mean for them. This is true, for example, of the long story of the Prodigal Son, which the New Revised Standard Version more helpfully titles 'The Parable of the Prodigal and His Brother' (Luke 15.11–31). The father in the story goes in turn to each of his two sons. First he runs to meet his younger son, to welcome him back home from his mis-spent time in a far country. Then, towards the end of the story, he goes to his elder son to plead with him to come and join the feast in honour of his younger brother. Do the father's pleadings succeed? Does the elder brother join the celebration? We are not told. Rather, we are left to put ourselves in the elder brother's place, to hear the request not to be grudging about God's gener-osity to others as addressed not just to the elder brother, but to us, and then to make our own response.

It can be quite difficult to live with uncertainty in this kind of way. Some of the parables of Jesus have quite lengthy explana-tions attached to them (the Parable of the Sower in Mark 4 is one example; another is the Parable of the Dishonest Manager in Luke 16). Some biblical scholars think the explanations do not quite fit the stories and that they were added by the Gos-pel writers who wanted to wrap things up neatly. Be that as it may, the temptation to do so in preaching should be resisted. If the subject matter of preaching is God's gracious *invitation* to faith and discipleship, the preacher needs to remember that the response to an invitation can only be given by those to whom it is addressed. If the preacher tries to close it off the invitation may not be heard at all.

9

Variety in Preaching

Every preacher begins as someone who listens to other people's preaching, perhaps for many years. As a result, we probably have an idea in our minds of what a good sermon should be like. Hopefully this will be because we have been personally helped and encouraged by such sermons. We are unlikely to have ever undertaken an analysis of *why* we find some sermons helpful and others less so or even not at all, though such an analysis is worth the novice preacher spending some time on. We will probably discover that the sermons that speak most directly to us are those that deal with those concerns about Christian discipleship and life in general that are uppermost in our minds at any given time; this would not be a surprising conclusion. We might then go on to recognize that other people in the congregation will have needs and concerns that differ from ours and it is therefore likely that they will find help and inspiration in the sort of preaching that makes less appeal to us personally. When we put these two simple reflections side by side it becomes obvious that all congregations need to experience variety in preaching if the opportunity to meet with God through the sermon is to be fully realized.

Variety on a Sunday

Some local churches are pastorates, or virtually so. Except for periods when the regular preacher is on holiday, or perhaps when some special occasion in the life of the church is being celebrated, the congregation hears the same preacher Sunday by Sunday. Other churches, especially larger ones, may have a small team of people who undertake the preaching; there may be a team vicar who takes the lion's share but with a non-stipendiary minister and/or a reader contributing on a regular basis. Other churches, especially those in a United Reformed Church group, a Methodist circuit or a group of rural Anglican parishes, have the minister or priest in pastoral charge preaching to them perhaps once a month, with the remaining services being taken by other people both lay and ordained. Those congregations will hear a greater variety of voices. It can be quite important for preachers to be aware of their particular situation. The more often they preach to any one congregation the more alert they should be to that congregation's need for variety.

But there are other reasons, of equal or greater importance, for making sure that we are attentive to the need for variety. The picture we hold in our own minds of what constitutes an ideal sermon can become a kind of goal at which to aim. That is not a bad thing in itself, but it can prove disastrous if the outcome is that we always preach in the same manner (because that is what appeals to us) or about the same subjects (because they are of most interest to us). We can then find ourselves, entirely unwittingly, preaching to please ourselves. While it is true, as has been said, that the preacher is always the first hearer of his or her sermon, it is certainly never intended for the preacher alone. In any case, to preach in the same way or about the same things for any length of time quickly leads to staleness and boredom, which our hearers will very speedily become aware of, even if we are not. For our own sake, as well as for that of our hearers, we need to deliberately cultivate variety in a number of different ways. Variety *can* be cultivated; it is not all that difficult provided we begin with what is familiar and are not afraid, once we have gained some confidence, to try new things.

Variety in content and style

There is a golden rule about writing sermons and it is this: the content must always determine the shape and structure. This is not always appreciated by fledgling preachers, because it can appear much easier and safer to begin with the structure. Especially at the beginning of a preaching ministry the task of saying something worthwhile for the congregation can feel so overwhelming that we understandably look for ways of setting limits to the task. Beginning with the structure can certainly help to do that. If you have a simple structure in mind (maybe the fairly common one of introduction, three points and a conclusion), that seems to reduce the work to be done to manageable proportions. It suggests that what you have to do is to jot down the headings on your computer screen or piece of paper and then think of suitable material to go under each one. It probably ensures that you don't ramble on and hopefully that you stop when you have reached the end. So a simple structure can appear like a lifeline to be gratefully grasped by a struggling preacher. Paradoxically, if we work with the same template on each occasion we become confident and proficient at doing it and it may then become a habit that forces all our sermons into the same mould. This produces preaching that is often static and dull and sometimes inappropriate. If the structure is predictable members of the congregation begin to think they know what is coming next – and they may be right. Even worse is the fact that by pushing our material into a predetermined pattern we distort it and do not allow it to speak to us. If it does not speak to us it cannot speak through us to others. What possible reason could there be for preaching, say, a three-point sermon about a story, such as one of the parables of Jesus?

One response to this dilemma is to engage in a serious study of what sorts of sermon structures suit different kinds of materials and contents. Some of the major textbooks about preaching choose to approach things in this way. They also analyse the manner in which people hear different kinds of materials and how adults learn, in the widest sense of that word. The results are often both fascinating and impressive, though they can frighten beginners to death by making it appear that good preaching is beyond the reach of all but the most skilled communicators. However, there are good grounds for questioning whether they might not be approaching the issue from the wrong direction. At one level preaching is certainly a craft, and one that involves skills being learned and honed over the years. But good sermons also have to have a considerable measure of spontaneity about them. That doesn't mean they should be improvised on the spot (which is almost always a recipe for disaster), but it does mean that they should never appear to be calculated or written to a formula, no matter how complex and intellectually satisfying. The necessary spontaneity arises out of the way in which the imagination of the preacher has been gripped and fired by the message that is being delivered. The sermon is not an academic exercise, it is a message from the living God that comes through real human beings and is delivered to real human beings. The preacher is certainly charged with giving that message coherence and structure, but the shaping has to be appropriate to the material and the end result something that can be delivered with conviction.

This really means having the courage to begin with the intended content, those materials that are to hand, and letting them determine the shape and structure. It is probably slightly too simple to say that if we get the content right the structure will take care of itself, but it is near enough to the truth to serve as a working assumption.

Types of sermons

This is a somewhat misleading subheading, which has been used only because no suitable alternative comes readily to mind. In truth, almost no sermon ever fits neatly into only one category. Most sermons include sufficiently diverse elements to warrant them being categorized in a number of different ways. So they should; it is one of the qualities that make for lively preaching. However, provided that caveat is borne in mind, it will not hurt to reflect on some of the types of sermon that can be preached.

The biblical sermon

Here is another unsatisfactory subheading! It was noted in Chapter 3 that preaching will normally be closely related to one or more of the biblical readings, because those readings are witnesses to the Word of God, Jesus Christ, whom we are called to preach. In that very important sense all sermons ought to be biblically based. Some, however, will deliberately set out to explain the meaning of the scriptural reading, or perhaps a verse within it, and to explore its relevance to Christian living today. This kind of preaching, once hugely popular and still much valued in some circles, can be called a 'biblical sermon' in a more specialized sense. It ought not to be neglected by the contemporary preacher. Its great virtue is that when it is done properly it helps worshippers to understand the importance of biblical material and its continuing significance in the life of faith. In an age of lamentable ignorance of the Scriptures, even within the Church, that is a very significant thing for the preacher to engage with.

Doing it well is not as scary as we might at first imagine. We do not have to be experts on the biblical text, though we do need to have done our homework, consulted the work of those who *are* experts and prayed that God's true message will shine through for us and our hearers. It is often during preliminary work on the sermon, while paying close attention to the text and consulting the commentaries, that the conviction comes that a particular passage lends itself to being directly expounded. So we are led by the reading itself into preaching this type of sermon on a particular occasion.

This kind of sermon (often called 'expository preaching') used to be a great deal more popular than it is today. During its heyday many examples were published. Reading them suggests that most preachers who practised it adopted a fairly standard sequence. First they offered background information that the congregation needed to know, then they explained what the passage or verse actually meant (clause by clause, verse by verse or even word by word, as appropriate) and finally they tried to make it clear what significance the passage still offered for Christian faith and life. There is nothing very much wrong with that kind of progression except that it requires a fairly sustained capacity on the part of the hearers to hold information in their minds and to follow a continuous argument. In a soundbite age the preacher can no longer take either of those things for granted. But a little reflection will suggest that there are other ways of expounding a biblical passage. For the most part these will be variants on a process of weaving together the two elements of what, on the one hand, the writer meant by the words he wrote and of how, on the other, we may live out those truths in daily living. Preachers who attempt this kind of preaching must discover themselves what sort of methodology feels comfortable to them.

Perhaps the point needs to be made that such preaching is only biblical (and indeed is only preaching) when it includes consideration of the issues around what the passage or verse means for us today. If we stop at imparting information about what the text means we have merely an essay in biblical interpretation rather than a sermon. It might be fascinating and interesting, but it is unlikely to be a message from God.

The topical sermon

An observation frequently met with in writings about preaching is that the preacher needs to have 'the Bible in one hand and the newspaper in the other'. This is said to have originated with the theologian Karl Barth but has been repeated so often that it has become almost proverbial among preachers. Its now commonplace nature does not make it any the less true (though we might want to substitute the television for the newspaper). It emphasizes the importance of biblical teaching being related to the real world in which we live. But it does raise the interesting question of whether a sermon might *begin* from the television or newspaper rather than the Bible. This isn't about whether the opening sentence might refer to a contemporary event rather than the Bible – we can take that for granted – but about whether the sermon can be essentially brought into being by what is in the news rather than what is in the readings for the day. The obvious answer is that indeed it can and on occasion it must be.

It would be inconceivable, surely, for a sermon not to deal quite directly with some great world event that has dominated the news during the previous week and that has profoundly affected the way in which everybody gathered in church on the Sunday morning understands the world in which they live. Although the media are sometimes prone to exaggeration, events do occur that change the world, or people's perceptions of it, and if the preacher has nothing to say about them, that is in itself a signal that the Christian faith is irrelevant to the things that most affect us. So those who found themselves preaching on the Sunday after 11 September 2001 (following what all of us now call in American fashion 9/11) could hardly avoid dealing with the issues that act of terrorism aroused, even though its implications had scarcely begun to sink in. To have ignored it would have been a clear dereliction of duty. That, of course, was an event with international implications that are ongoing. There can, similarly, be national events to which the same importance can be attached. And, since churches are called to minister to the local communities in which they are set, some events that take place in that setting can and should carry similar weight. In such situations a sermon can indeed legitimately be generated by the news rather than by the readings for the day.

There are several things that a preacher needs to remember in those circumstances. He is unlikely to be an expert on the issues concerned, but can take comfort from the fact that the congregation is not expecting him to be. The preacher is not a newspaper columnist, but members of the congregation will already have more than enough of such comments to digest after lunch if they take a Sunday paper. What fellow worshippers are looking for on such an occasion is a Christian perspective – which is not the same as a Christian answer. The preacher, struggling with issues beyond his (or anyone's) immediate comprehension, will not pretend to have simple answers to complicated questions, or rush to judgement. Almost certainly the great need will be to address with a gospel word the emotions that the horrific events have aroused: fear, anxiety, anger, disbelief and grief.

When circumstances require the preacher to begin from the story in the news care needs to be taken to ensure that the sermon is still biblical. The lectionary readings may well not prove to be appropriate for the occasion, though this should not be assumed automatically, because sometimes they may be very apposite. However, when they are not, the preacher is justified in searching for readings from the Bible that speak to the occasion, and using those instead. This is quite different from the preacher deciding what he or she would like to preach about and then finding readings that match; that is normally bad practice, because it makes the Scriptures a prop rather than the foundation. But when external events effectively choose the preacher's subject for her it is perfectly honourable to search the Bible for passages that speak to that situation.

The apologetic sermon

This might appear to be a rather strange subheading! We usually use the word 'apologetic' to describe something for which an apology needs to be made. No doubt apologies ought sometimes to be offered for the sermons we preach, but that is not its meaning here. In this context it refers to a discipline known as 'apologetics', which is about making a systematic defence of something (in this case the Christian faith) against those who attack it. Christian apologetics takes its cue from the instruction given to believers in 1 Peter 3.15: 'Always be ready to make your defence to anyone who demands from you an accounting for the hope that is in you.' Even though by the nature of things we cannot ultimately 'prove' the truth of Christianity according to the laws of logic or science, this does not mean that it is intellectually disreputable. The task of defending the faith is a very important one, since it is under attack at a number of different levels.

For most of the latter half of the twentieth century the general public and media attitude towards religion was largely one of indifference. Churchgoers were viewed by the liberal secular establishment as a bit odd but, by and large, harmless enough. The Church was sometimes a bit of a nuisance, but most of the time could simply be assumed to be irrelevant to life as people usually lived it. With some notable exceptions most agnostics and atheists could not become sufficiently excited about their agnosticism or atheism to bother arguing an anti-religious case. Since fewer people were going to church as the years went by it was, in any case, not worth doing so; religion in Britain looked set to pass away quietly.

What appears to have changed this as we go into the twenty-first century is the belated recognition that a significant number of British citizens actually take their religion very seriously indeed and some of them find it quite difficult to live comfortably in a secular, pluralist society. They just happen to be Muslims rather than Christians. It has become demonstrably inaccurate to say that religion is irrelevant in the modern world; it is clearly extremely relevant and, in some of its more extreme manifestations, rather dangerous. So for some politicians and media commentators religion, including Christianity, has become a baleful influence that needs to be actively opposed. We can see this from numerous newspaper articles, and also from radio and television programmes. In an edition of BBC Radio 4's *Any Questions?* broadcast on Holy Saturday, 7 April 2007, there was a question about why there is a growing culture of violence among young people. None of the panellists even hinted at the decline of the Church's influence over young people as one possible contributory factor. The next questioner asked whether the panel agreed with Karl Marx that religion is the 'opium of the people'. Two of the panellists attacked Christianity as a more or less dangerous delusion, though one of the two said she enjoyed the cultural spin-offs such as church buildings and church music. The third panellist (Tony Benn) spoke of his admiration for the teaching of Jesus and the remaining panel member described himself as a churchgoer and defended Christianity on the rather dubious grounds that it offers us comfort in a harsh world. What was notable, and new, was the significant amount of applause the audience gave to those who were openly hostile to the Christian faith. Those who listen to our sermons hear and see such programmes. They also live and work alongside people who hold such views and are, increasingly it seems, giving voice to them. Where will they hear a defence of their faith, if not from those of us who preach?

Sometimes there are quite specific issues that need to be dealt with in some appropriate way. It is in the nature of the media to enjoy sensational stories, and sometimes those concern Christianity. From time to time a scientist or archaeologist will announce seemingly convincing proof that Jesus never lived, did not die on the cross, or did not rise from the dead, or something else appropriately sensational. Such stories usually go away quickly enough, but perhaps not before they have unsettled the minds of some believers. The most difficult things to deal with are those that, for whatever reason, grip the public's collective imagination. One very notable instance was the publication in 2003 of Dan Brown's best-selling *The Da Vinci Code* and the film that followed in 2006. The book is, of course, a novel. But it suggests, among other things, that Jesus was a radically different person from the one portrayed in the New Testament and, indeed, that the accounts in the Gospels are quite misleading. It is a conspiracy-theory novel, which postulates that the 'real' facts about Jesus, the disciples and others have been deliberately covered up by the Church, which has practised deception on everybody for over two thousand years. We live in a free society and Mr Brown is entitled to write whatever kind of novel he pleases. The difficulty is that very many people, especially in an age of widespread religious ignorance, have no easy way of separating the facts from the fiction. To many people the fantasy world of *The Da Vinci Code* appears to be a perfectly plausible reconstruction of the life of Jesus and certainly much spicier and more interesting than the New Testament. What this does is to create a kind of 'feeling in the air' that Mr Brown's imaginings are at least as plausible as the evidence of history. If they are, then Christian faith lies in ruins. Again there are those in our congregations who live and work alongside people who think like that. Where will they receive reassurance about the intellectual, historical and doctrinal foundations of their faith if not from those of us who preach?

Preaching apologetic sermons, or including apologetic material in the sermons we preach, might seem a somewhat intimidating prospect and perhaps it is, especially for beginners. But such preaching often relates to specific issues or controversies and there are almost always scholarly resources that can provide us with the materials we need at the time. Something more will be said about this in the resources section.

Sermons on social issues

The Church is generally good at raising social issues. Over many years such things as reports and speeches by church leaders have offered serious analysis of the problems that exist within our society, both drawing attention to them and, quite often, suggesting directions in which solutions might be sought. Sometimes these activities annoy governments, who would rather the Church kept quiet. The Church is concerned about social issues because the God who is revealed to us in Jesus Christ is God of the whole universe. Christianity is most certainly about our personal individual relationship with God, but that is only the beginning. The Lordship of Christ means that the abundant life that Jesus said he came to bring (John 10.10) should be available in equal measure to every human being. That, in turn, means those who seek for and then speak God's message being concerned about the conditions that blight lives and restrict human flourishing. Racism, crime and violence, unemployment, bad housing, educational inequalities, injustice, exploitation and the problems of asylum seekers, to mention but a few of the social evils that afflict us, are inescapably the concern of the Church and therefore of the preacher. So too, of course, are the really big international issues, such as Third World development, global warming and climate change.

In this situation there are two basic traps into which the unwary preacher can easily fall. The first is to acknowledge the responsibility, but to do nothing about it because we are too scared to tackle it. This is understandable because many of the topics are simply huge. We are surrounded by constant debate about most of them and we are almost certainly not experts on any of them. Where would we begin to tread in such a minefield? The second trap is to become so immersed in the issues that we become single-issue preachers who rarely preach about anything else and whose sermons turn into lectures about them, replete with reams of statistics and rather a lot of the kind of nagging that merely results in congregations feeling guilty. If it is not the preacher's job to give the impression by never mentioning them that God doesn't care about the world's problems, neither is it the preacher's job to create guilt-ridden Christians.

What we ought to try to do as preachers is to make connections for people between the nature of the God we worship as revealed in Jesus Christ and the issue with which we are dealing. How does God invite us to become involved – by our prayers, by giving, by campaigning, by changing our lifestyle? Dealing with social issues comes more easily to some preachers than to others, but it must never be social comment with a religious tinge. At its heart should be an encounter with God's grace which changes preacher and hearers alike.

Sermons on spirituality

One of the most disturbing aspects of the Church's reputation is how few people seem to make any connection between the Church and what is broadly called 'spirituality'. There is a great deal of interest in our society in spirituality in the broadest sense, even if the form and content of some of it strikes us as somewhat weird and wonderful, but this has not been reflected in a growing interest in Christianity. How have we reached the position where, after more than 1500 years of Christian history and tradition in the British Isles, there is a rising interest in Paganism and Wicca? The answer to that question is doubtless complicated, but part of it may be about the way the Church has so often presented itself and has been both seen and experienced by others. Perhaps we are paying the price for being seen purely as an institution, at times in the past a large, hierarchical and powerful institution, unduly cerebral and concerned rather more with theological disputes, social issues, morals and looking after its own interests than with spirituality.

Preachers have an important part to play in ensuring that the Church does not unwittingly collude with this lack of understanding. Christian spirituality is very much richer and deeper – and more securely founded – than most of the options on offer elsewhere, and the preacher should try to build up confidence about this. During its long history the Church at its best has developed numerous different ways in which people can pray, meditate, engage in spiritual reading, learn to know themselves and, above all, discover both how to meet with God and how to proceed when God seems to be absent. In doing so it has drawn heavily on its Jewish roots and even, at times, on some spiritual traditions found in other faiths, which have been 'Christianized'. As it is often defined today, spirituality does not necessarily involve connecting with God, but the Christian tradition can show up the shallowness of that. When one beggar shows another beggar where to find bread it is in order that the bread may be eaten and the hunger satisfied. At the heart of Christian spirituality is the famous statement addressed to God by the Church Father Augustine of Hippo (354–430): 'You move us to delight in praising you; for you have formed us for yourself and our hearts are restless till they find rest in you.'

Yet how often do we hear, or preach, sermons on issues of spirituality? At the very least worshippers might be given help to understand what they are doing when they take part in a church service week by week. What does it mean for a human being to praise and adore, to acknowledge someone or something outside and beyond ourselves – which is what we do in our hymns and prayers? Why is listening to a reading from the Bible both like and unlike listening to a reading from any other book? How do the prayers we make in our hearts relate to the words of prayer we utter? How do bread and wine, which are both fruits of the earth and that which human hands have made, connect us to both God and human work, so that we respect the creation because we honour the creator? The liturgy alone provides us with an abundance of material on spirituality through which we can hear God's gracious invitation to deeper faith.

These days most people who are at worship in church on a Sunday are there because they want to be rather than out of habit or social custom. But some of them may not have delved very deeply into the reasons why they want to be there – they just know that they do! The preacher who can help people to make connections between what they do in church and the spirituality that expresses the deepest desires of the human psyche will be doing a considerable service. And if (which happens more often than we sometimes suppose) the congregation includes someone who is interested or curious but not a regular church-goer, he or she will discover, hopefully with surprise and delight, that Christianity offers a spirituality that is deeply satisfying.

Have a go?

There are, of course, numerous other kinds of sermons than those that have been discussed. Because we are all different (and we recall that if God has called us to preach that is in part because of who we are and what we can offer), we find some sorts of sermons very much easier to prepare than we do others. The wise old piece of advice to 'pray as you can and not as you can't' applies equally to preaching: we should preach as we can and not as we can't, at least at the beginning. As we grow in experience and in a proper kind of confidence, the kind of preaching we feel we can't do when we start may well cease to appear impossible. All things, we are told, are possible to God!

Variety of occasion

When children are present

Although there are many churches where, sadly, children are rarely present at services of public worship, this is not the story everywhere. There are congregations that run a regular Sunday School or Junior Church and where children may worship alongside the adults for a time – usually before they leave for their groups but sometimes joining the congregation towards the end of the service. At one time it was very common for the preacher to be asked to supply a children's address, but these are less common than once they were, largely because they can prove confusing to the children when they deal with a topic different from the one that will be explored in the Junior Church or Sunday School.

Churches that are fortunate enough to have a number of children and young people often hold 'All-Age Worship' or 'Family Services' at stated intervals, when the whole of the church family worships together for the entire time. The preacher who ministers in a church or group of churches where this happens will find him- or herself being asked to preach on the occasion sooner or later. There are, broadly speaking, two possible ways for us to approach this scenario, one of them perhaps works better than the other, though it has to be said that neither of them is entirely satisfactory.

The first method is to deliver just one sermon or address, largely aimed at the children. The main advantages are that delivering one sermon rather than two is helpful if the overall length of the service is to be kept fairly short, as it should be for all-age worship, and that only one lot of preparation is required on the preacher's part. There are several drawbacks. The occasion is supposed to be all-age worship, not children's worship. In any case, since children learn and understand differently at different ages, at what age group among those children present does the preacher aim? In practice, those who use this method tend to aim at somewhere around Year 7, but this can leave the younger children bewildered and the older ones bored.

The second approach is to deliver two sermons, one directed towards the younger children and the other for the older children and the adults. This makes slightly better sense from an educationalist's point of view, though it is demanding on the preacher's preparation time. Both addresses will, of course, need to be quite short. The one designed for the older children and the adults should probably last no longer than about six or seven minutes. The preacher needs to make every effort to ensure that the language that is used is as accessible as possible to young people and that material, including illustrations, does not presuppose an adult experience or understanding of life. That is not to say that we have to avoid difficult or demanding subjects. The media frequently portray young people as shallow and as interested only in themselves. This is quite untrue. Children of secondary school age and even younger are very aware of the world's problems and often passionate about changing the world in which they live. Many of them have access through the internet to significant information and resources. What they do not have, as yet, are the life experiences that enable them to understand the issues quite in the way in which adults understand them. But it is very important that preachers do not give children and young people the impression that the Christian faith has nothing to say about significant issues and problems. It is also worth reflecting on whether, given the amount of anti-Christian propaganda many young people are subjected to, the short and punchy sermons we produce for all-age worship might not often have an apologetic element to them. The aim, as always, is to deliver a message that builds up the faith of the hearers and conveys something of the vibrancy of belief in a living God.

Weekday services

It is a fascinating and encouraging fact that recent research has shown that weekday services are the largest single growth point for attendance at worship across all the mainstream denominations. Given the way in which the character of Sunday has changed in the last few years and looks set to go on changing, this may well continue to be the case. Preachers, both ordained and lay, are increasingly likely to find themselves involved in leading such worship. Then the question arises: should they include preaching? It cannot be answered with a simple yes or no, because there is a huge variety of midweek worship currently on offer and a great deal of proper experimentation to discover what works best. But if, as was argued in Chapter 1, sermons change lives, open the door to new experiences of God's grace and love, evoke commitment, deepen faith and challenge limitations, the presumption at least must surely be that it is done, however briefly, in every act of worship in which the Scriptures are read.

About the only thing midweek services all have in common is that they are generally much shorter than a standard Sunday morning service in church, with about half an hour appearing to be the norm. Clearly, a 15-minute sermon, or even a 10-minute one, is disproportionate in that context. But who says that a sermon has to be 15 or 20 minutes long? It is perfectly possible to preach, and to say something significant, in five or even in three minutes, and we need to develop the techniques through which to do so. Such a sermon probably needs to have an attention-grabbing opening, after which it should aim to hold the attention of the hearers for the whole of its length (something we would be unwise to reckon on for our usual preaching). It might make just one or two quick points about the biblical reading, then offer a couple of sentences about its significance for today. It could end with a question that invites the hearers to reflect on how God is inviting them to respond, or in some other equally open-ended way. It would be easy to dismiss this as soundbite preaching. Perhaps it is, but it is a style of preaching that fits our age, and we need to learn how to do it.

Services for interest groups

Even in our multicultural society a surprising number of organizations still ask to hold a service in church either on an annual basis or to mark a particular anniversary or other occasion for celebration. If we have been asked to preach at one of these services it is probably either because of a particular position we hold within the life of the Church or in view of some personal connection we have with the charity or other organization concerned. It goes without saying that as preachers we will honour the reason for the service being held and do some appropriate research into the aims and achievements of the organization that has requested it. It is equally important for us to remember that in this setting the aim of preaching remains the same as it does in a straightforward Sunday service. We are not there to deliver a eulogy or tribute to the organization, but rather to seek to discern how the values of God's kingdom are advanced by its work and to invite people to celebrate that as a gift of God.

Preachers need to take particular care with Remembrance Sunday. Services on Remembrance Sunday morning are sometimes held in the open air, perhaps around a local cenotaph, but also inside church buildings. Very many preachers find that this responsibility comes their way sooner or later. On those occasions a sizeable proportion of the congregation may be made up of members of the Royal British Legion, some of whom may not come to Christian worship at any other time, but who are there for the entirely honourable reason that they wish to remember comrades who perished in war. The preacher often has to walk a tightrope, and some fall off. The present writer recalls hearing a sermon delivered on such an occasion by a long-retired bishop who made frequent references to 'our kith and kin' but none at all to Jesus and only one, right at the end, to God! Here too, the preacher's aim is to speak of God and of the things of God within the context of the particular remembering in which those present are engaged.

Learning to preach in a number of different ways and responding to the stimulus of preaching on varied occasions are among the things that keep preachers fresh and alert.

Postscript

The story is told of a preacher returning to his home after morning service one Sunday and telling the friends who had just arrived for lunch how extremely well received his sermon had been. 'What was it about?' one of them asked. 'Humility,' he replied. The tale encapsulates a dilemma with which every preacher is familiar. From the moment we begin to preach we seek to do it as well as we possibly can. It is, after all, a high calling. We dare not preach in a slapdash, careless or casual way, for it is the very word of God that we are handling. We would not preach without proper preparation, which involves substantial time in studying the Scriptures and collecting fresh resources in the areas of Bible and theology. We will not preach without prayer, both in the actual preparation and, as we deliver the sermon, that God will use our poor words to awaken and deepen faith and commitment among those who listen to us. Preaching is our offering of gratitude to God, our response to all that God has done for us.

The better we become at preaching the more our congregations are likely to comment appreciatively on our efforts. Those who are not called to preach can have no idea how humbling it is when somebody who has just listened to us says something like, 'Thank you for what you said; it spoke to my situation.' That is an amazing thing to have happen, for preaching does change lives and we, it seems, are sometimes the medium through which that occurs. False modesty is not a virtue, though humility is. If we are conscious of having done our best and if it appears that the result on a particular occasion has been significant, even if only for one person, there is a proper pride that may be taken in that. The warm glow that praise from others induces in us should be offered up to God in prayer. But, as hardly needs saying, we do not preach as an act of self-aggrandizement, to collect for ourselves the reputation of being a good preacher or to win praise of any kind. The calling is from God, the message is from God, the glory must all be for God as well. Preachers do well when they take as their motto the words of John the Baptist concerning Jesus: 'He must increase, but I must decrease' (John 3.30). Sometimes the best the preacher can do is not to get in God's way too much.

In fact, improper pride is not often a problem for preachers. Yes, it is true, astonishingly so in fact, that God has called us to this work. Yes, it is true that the God who calls us also enables us to discover rich resources for what we are doing. Yes, it is true that we are, for the most part, ministering to gracious and kindly people who encourage us and uphold us with their prayers. But for most of us none of those truths ever quite banish the feeling we have as we preach that we could have done better than we did. This is not because we have an ambition to preach some notional perfect sermon (now that really *would* be pride!); rather, it is a pointer to the vast, immeasurable treasure and mystery of our faith. How could any human being, even those who are much more eloquent than we are, possibly begin to do justice to the Christian story? How could words, even carefully fashioned and prayed-over words, ever be adequate to speak about a God who is Father, Son and Holy Spirit, whose love for humanity is shown in incarnation, in cross and in resurrection? How could we ever sound the depths of divine love, understand the great puzzle of evil and suffering or say with confidence what life with God in heaven will be like? *Of course* we could have done better than we did! But that is no reason for despair. The miracle

133

of it all is that God takes the little we bring and somehow it is enough. A few loaves and fishes become a feast for all. Truly the glory belongs to God.

In his book *The Word and the Words* (Epworth Press, 1975) the preacher, writer and broadcaster Colin Morris magnificently sums up the preacher's task in this way:

> Let every preacher take heart from the fact that Shakespeare wrote over 150 sonnets attempting to capture the essence of Love in words and had to confess his failure. But he made beautiful music in the process. Possibly that is the best the greatest preacher can do – fail magnificently and in so doing testify to the glory of the God who eludes us in our eloquence and yet is hauntingly present in our silences.

Amen to that.

Resources

This section offers a select list of resources, intended to help those who are beginning a preaching ministry to move on to the next stage. For the most part they relate to the issues around preaching that have been explored in this book. Although the main body of the book has tried hard not to presuppose any prior theological study on the part of the reader, some of the resources listed here do make that supposition. Most of the books listed are in print and available from booksellers at the time of this book's publication. However, some out-of-print books are mentioned if they are judged to be worth searching for through second-hand booksellers.

The internet is a considerable and growing resource for preachers, including those who are thinking about beginning to preach. There are some excellent websites available that can help to resource a preaching ministry. However, a word of caution is necessary. It is not always easy to establish the source, and therefore the credibility or intellectual respectability, of some websites. For example, if you were looking for material to help you with preaching at Christmas about the incarnation you might try putting 'incarnation' into a search engine. You might then find yourself logging on to a website run by one of those fringe or sub-Christian organizations that do not share the orthodox Christian understanding of incarnation, though the website might well be set up in a way which attempts to conceal that fact. Granted, you would probably work it out after a while, but it could be quite confusing at first. And there are plenty of websites set up by individuals who have strong but extremely unorthodox views on all sorts of theological and biblical subjects. It is not always easy to recognize them unless you have sufficient prior theological training.

One way of being reasonably sure that the material you are accessing represents mainstream Christian thought is to make use of those that originate from respectable universities in the UK and from universities and seminaries belonging to the mainstream denominations in the USA. If your search brings up an article in the free online encyclopaedia Wikipedia you can usually be sure that the information it provides will be accurate and reasonably objective. The articles are contributed by scholarly enthusiasts and are open to being edited by others. So, to use the example above, if you put 'Incarnation' into the search engine it will bring up a Wikipedia entry on the subject. There is (at the time of writing – a proviso that usually needs to be made about websites) a brief description of what Christianity believes about incarnation. Clicking on the 'Christianity' link then takes you to a very substantial article that will tell you very much more than you probably need to know, but it is certainly reliable. Always bear in mind that what you read in Wikipedia is not a piece of creative theology, it is an entry in an encyclopaedia, which means that it aims at objectivity and neutrality and usually achieves it. You will not find anything in the Wikipedia entry on incarnation that argues for the truth of the doctrine – that is the preacher's task! Articles are mostly at a fairly demanding intellectual level.

The Bible

The publishers Lion Books have done a first-rate job in producing highly accessible books on the Bible. David Winter, *The Espresso Bible: The Bible in Sips* (Oxford, Lion Books, 2007) uses actual biblical text with linking and explanatory comments to give a summary of the Bible as a whole. Those who would find it helpful to have an overview of the entire Bible that is written in an entirely non-technical way and includes cartoons and graphics, could hardly do better than Simon Jenkins, *The Bible from Scratch* (Oxford, Lion Books, 2004). A different kind of perspective on the Bible can be found in Walter Wangerin, *The Book of God* (Oxford, Lion Books, 1998). The subtitle, 'The Bible as a Novel', sums up the approach. It is very readable and does an excellent job in bringing the biblical characters to life. This certainly conveys the larger picture. John Goldingay, *How to Read the Bible*, (London, SPCK, 1997) is more conventional than the preceding titles. It is based on very sound scholarship from a mainstream evangelical stable and, although not difficult to read, is more serious in tone. Any of the above books would help considerably in acquiring a sense of how the various parts of the Bible fit together, including the way in which the story of God's dealings with the people of Israel forms the essential background to the story of Jesus.

The issue of how Christians actually use the Bible as a source of authority for faith and conduct is a complex one and there is a vast literature associated with it at every level. A provocative and challenging way into the topic can be found in Stephen Dawes, *Why Bible Believing Methodists Shouldn't Eat Black Pudding*. This is now available as a free download on www.swmtc.org.uk/tutors%20handouts.htm. Most of the published material deals with the use of the Bible in relation to one particular issue or else assumes a fairly high level of theological education. There would appear to be no reliable and trustworthy online resources in this area, though a number do offer basic biblical information.

Once a new preacher has worked through some of the ways of getting to grips with the biblical text that are suggested in this book, it might be appropriate to tackle more advanced writing on the subject. It would be hard to do better than Carl R. Holla-day and John H. Hayes, *Biblical Exegesis: A Beginner's Handbook* (London, SCM Press, 1988). This will open up new perspectives on how to study the Scriptures. D. E. R. Isitt, *The Light of the Living: Studies in the Interpretation of Scripture* (London, Epworth Press, 1989), which explains the 'close attention to the text' method of approaching the Bible and offers a number of worked-out examples, is now out of print but worth searching for.

Those who are looking for lectionary commentaries have quite a wide choice. Three volumes published by the Epworth Press between them cover the Revised Common Lectionary readings for all three years. The general title is *Companion to the Revised Common Lectionary: Mining the Meaning*. That for Year A (vol. 6) is by Harry McKeating, that for Year B (vol. 7) by Michael Townsend and that for Year C (vol. 8) by Sandy Williams. Written by experienced preachers, these volumes provide reliable material to help preachers get into the texts, interweaving explanation and application for each passage. A single-volume lectionary commentary of considerable quality is Reginald H. Fuller and Daniel Westberg, *Preaching the Lectionary: The Word of God for the Church Today* (Minnesota, Liturgical Press, 3rd edition 2006). The American context sometimes influences its tone, and the commentary material is slightly more academic than some will wish, but it is well worth acquiring.

There are a number of websites that offer lectionary commentary material (unfortunately, some of them also offer complete sermons!). Some of the material is free and some is only available on subscription, though free samples of the latter can usually be inspected. There are plenty of links to other websites claiming to offer helpful material, and readers will need to check them out for themselves. Many of them originate in America and there are some disadvantages with these, especially for the novice preacher: a slightly different version of the lectionary is sometimes used, it is not always clear from which denomination the material originates, so some of the doctrinal material may not be what you are looking for, and if you follow the links for long enough you can come to some moderately eccentric things!

Possibly the most helpful online resource is www.textweek. com – though it is important not to be confused by the plethora of links it displays immediately on entry. You need to click on the date for which you want help (Saints Days are included as well as Sundays). Then, under the heading 'Reading and Studying the Text This Week', scroll down to 'Commentary, Exegesis and Sermon Preparation' and click on 'Preaching Helps'. This site uses commentary material from a wide range of authors in many denominations. Naturally, they vary in quality and helpfulness, but in general they are excellent at providing the preacher with ways into the biblical texts. This site assumes that the Psalm that is provided each Sunday by the lectionary is one of the readings; strictly speaking it isn't. The normal practice is to use the Psalm in worship rather than to preach on it.

A website called lectionary.org offers material that is the work of Dick and Dale Kathleen Donovan, under the title of *Sermonwriter*. To access it, under 'Biblical Exegesis' click on 'English', which brings up a list of those biblical books for which commentary currently exists (new material is being added all the time). Click on the book you want and it will display a list of passages from that book on which material is available. The work is scholarly and reliable, sometimes a little bit more scholarly than the preacher who is just beginning needs, but always helpful. The typing is occasionally a little slapdash.

It should be the aim of every preacher to build up a modest library of commentaries on individual books of the Bible. They enable us to understand, and work with, books of the Bible as a whole, in a way that even the best lectionary commentaries can never do. A library of such commentaries, wisely chosen, can become a resource for years ahead. However, for a number of reasons it is quite difficult to list suitable commentaries. In part this is because there are so many of them and some extremely good ones are really written for scholars rather than preachers. At the other end of the scale there are commentaries that purport to offer basic guidance to preachers and others, but that rarely tell us anything we could not have worked out quite easily for ourselves. The ideal commentary for the preacher is one that helps to explain what the text actually means but in non-technical language so far as that can be done. It should not spoon-feed us with suggestions about how the text is relevant for us today, but good suggestions are always welcome!

The best way of building up such a resource is to pay an extended visit to a bookshop with a really good selection of commentaries and spend a lot of time dipping into them to see which ones look suitable. Unfortunately, that is not something that everyone is able to do, largely because such bookshops are regrettably thinner on the ground than they used to be. As a starter, here are some comments about a few commentary *series* where the general standard of writing is reliable and helpful, though it should be borne in mind that some individual volumes within the series may be below standard and others above. (1) The Peoples Bible Commentaries are published by the Bible Reading Fellowship and now cover the whole of the Bible. The general standard is fine, sometimes very good indeed. The snag is that they really are quite basic and do not always help with the most difficult passages. They might be a good starting-point but will probably need supplementing as a preaching ministry develops. (2) The NIV Application Commentaries are published by Zondervan in the USA, but widely available in the UK. Currently a fair proportion of the Bible is covered. There are some good volumes in this series, but it tends to be theologically and biblically conservative, which some will count a virtue. (3) The Epworth Commentaries are published by the Epworth Press and cover most parts of the Bible that are likely to be used in preaching. A few volumes are fairly technical, but most achieve their aim of being useful to the preacher. (4) Comparable to these are the New International Bible Commentaries published by Paternoster. Unfortunately, only a relatively small number of biblical books are dealt with, but there are some distinguished volumes in this series. (5) The Interpretation Commentaries are published by Westminster John Knox Press in the USA but reasonably readily available in the UK. These contain some very scholarly material, but the authors all make a real effort to write intelligibly for the non-specialist and specific attention is paid to the message that can be found in the passages being examined.

Theology and doctrine

This is quite a difficult area in which to suggest reliable resources because the needs of the preacher may, at least at first, be influenced by the doctrinal standards and theological outlook of the particular denomination to which he or she belongs. Denominational offices such as those for Anglican and Roman Catholic dioceses, Methodist districts and URC synods may well be able to provide information about whether these exist and how they may be obtained. Good websites offering reliable material are hard to locate. The Christian Enquiry Agency runs one on behalf of the major churches and it can be accessed at www.Christianity.org.uk but the information it provides is fairly limited and it is really intended for those making initial enquiries about Christianity.

There are several good books that the novice preacher would find useful. One is George Pattison, *A Short Course in Christian Doctrine* (London, SCM Press, 2005). Another, which as its title suggests explores Christian theology by using the Apostles' Creed, is Hans Küng, *Credo: The Apostles' Creed Explained for Today* (London, SCM Press, 1993).

Sermons on various subjects

When we want to include apologetic material in a sermon it is usually in response to a particular current issue or publication on which we may be anything but expert. The internet offers preachers the possibility of obtaining reliable scholarly material that has nevertheless been produced speedily as a Christian response. There is no alternative to using a search engine. So, for example, putting *Da Vinci Code* into Google Search will bring up a number of websites offering scholarly Christian comment on the issues. The reliable ones can usually be recognized from their reasoned and reasonable tone. Those that are mildly hysterical or abusive are better ignored.

There is a plethora of resources relating to the Christian response to all kinds of social issues. Although the social problem concerned may be of long-standing, the particular circumstances around it can change quite quickly. For this reason internet resources can be more useful than printed ones. Most major denominations conduct extensive research on major social issues, often resulting in reports and statements that can provide helpful background material for the preacher, with downloads sometimes being available. The simplest way of accessing this work is to visit the official national website for the denomination and follow appropriate links. In most cases the following websites apply to England or England and Wales, though there are usually links on them to the official sites for Scotland and Ireland if these are different:

The Baptist Union: www.baptist.org.uk
The Church of England: www.cofe.anglican.org
The Methodist Church: www.methodist.org.uk
The Roman Catholic Church: www.catholic-ew.org.uk
The United Reformed Church: www.urc.org.uk

Just as there are numerous expressions and out-workings of

Christian spirituality so there are many publications that deal with it. The most comprehensive source of reliable information is Philip Sheldrake, ed., *The New SCM Dictionary of Christian Spirituality* (London, SCM Press, 2005). It contains over 400 articles by leading scholars, but unfortunately it is an expensive volume and may provide more than the preacher initially needs. The book that it replaced on the publisher's list is Gordon S. Wakefield, ed., *A Dictionary of Spirituality* (London, SCM Press, 1983). This is now out of print and, although dated in some respects, can still be relied upon for basic information and is worth searching out second-hand. For those who wish to explore traditions of Christian spirituality in a more advanced way there is Cheslyn Jones, Geoffrey Wainwright and Edward Yarnold, eds, *The Study of Spirituality* (London, SPCK, 1986) which offers untold riches to the serious reader.

If this book has helped the reader to make up his or her mind about whether there is a sense of call to the preaching ministry and then to make an appropriate response, it will have done what the author hoped and intended in the writing of it. Of course, as the Introduction says, this is very much a first book about its subject. There are many other perspectives on preaching and, consequently, a considerable number of excellent books that will stimulate further thought and open up different perspectives. It was tempting to list some of them here, but it would not have been appropriate. This book is aimed at raising awareness of some of the issues that are significant at the beginning of a preaching ministry. Once those have been properly considered the important thing is to actually get started and then to continue the reflection in the light of the experience of testing the call.